Toni G. Boehm, Ph.D.

The
Power
of
yes

First Edition 2006
Second Edition 2007

Inner Visioning Press
430 Winnebago Dr.
Greenwood, MO. 64034
816-537-5254 (F)
816-537-7521 (B)

Published by Inner Visioning Press
Printed in the United States of America

The publisher wishes to gratefully acknowledge the
design work of Gail Ishmael, she is not only a graphic artist
she is a friend to Inner Visioning Press.

Library of Congress Card Number: 2001012345
The Power of YES! / Toni G. Boehm Ph. D.

ISBN 978-0-9701537-5-3

1. Self-Help   2. Body, Mind & Spirit   I. Title
The Power of YES!

Table of Contents

TABLE OF CONTENTS
DEDICATION AND ACKNOWLEDGMENTS

INTRODUCTION:

Soul-Searching: "What Do You Really Want for Your Life?"

What Do You Really Want For Your Life
The Cosmic 2x4 Experience
The Circle of 'Transformation': Intuit, Inquire, Imagine, Innovate, and Implement
A 'YES' Experience: The Circle of Transformation

CHAPTER 1: THE CIRCLE OF 'TRANSFORMATION': INTUIT

Are You Listening?

Change? Why Would I Want to do That?
A 'YES' Experience: Igniting the Spark
YES!
A 'YES' Experience: An Extraordinary Being
YES, an Affirmation
Dancing at the Edge of Mystery
A 'YES' Experience: Dancing at the Edge of Mystery

CHAPTER 2: THE CIRCLE OF 'TRANSFORMATION': INQUIRE

Self-Inquiry - A Journey Inward

Gear for the Journey
A 'YES' Experience: What If?
The Art of Asking 'Right' Questions
A 'YES' Experience: Self-Awareness - Who Am I?
Self-Inquiry: Who Am I?
A 'YES' Experience: Who Am I?-Meditation
A 'YES' Experience: One Desire
Self-Knowledge

CHAPTER 3: THE CIRCLE OF 'TRANSFORMATION': IMAGINE

"You are the Root Cause of Your Experience"

Stopping Negative Thoughts and Monkey Mind Chatter

Changing the Internal Dialogue

Imagine This-Conscious Choice Creates Conscious Transformation

A 'YES' Experience: Imagine Learning to Respond in New Ways

A 'YES' Experience: Imagine Slaying the Green-Eyed Monster

Imagine Poss-I-bility

A 'YES' Experience: Imagine Liberation From Limitation

CHAPTER 4: THE CIRCLE OF 'TRANSFORMATION': INNOVATE

"Reality is not as Reality is ...

Shifting Perceptions Creates New Realities

A 'YES' Experience: Taking Inventory-What Shaped My Perceptions

A 'YES' Experience: How Big Do You Dare to Dream?

CHAPTER 5: THE CIRCLE OF 'TRANSFORMATION': IMPLEMENT

Intention, Direction, and Attention Aligned With Focus, Clarity, & Purpose Create Authentic Actions

What Am I Implementing?

A 'YES' Experience: Shifting Behavior Patterns

Intention-What Did I Really Intend to Do?

A 'YES' Experience: My Intention Was To ...

Attention-On What Am I Focusing?

A 'YES' Experience: A Stretch!

Direct Your Mind and You Direct Your Life

A 'YES' Experience: 30 Day Authentic Action Plan

A 'YES' Experience: A Presence Pause

EPILOGUE: SOUL-SEARCHING'S

A 'YES' Experience: Healing Waters

SEVEN WEEK STUDY GUIDE

ENDNOTES

Dedication and Acknowledgments

Dedication

- To my husband, Jay, my partner in co-creation and friend.
- To my grandmother and grandfather, Laura and George, I am grateful for your wise counsel.
- To Dr. Bill Phaturos, my nephew, the Chiropractor. Your wise counsel was perfect.
- To my sister Rosalie, I appreciate your discerning eye; I love you.
- To my cousin Pam, thank you for always being there for me.
- To the rest of my family, I love you and the lessons you have shared with me!
- To the universal power of '**YES**,' and the Cosmic 2x4 that changed my life's direction.

Acknowledgments

- To Rev. Dr. Marj Britt, a mentor, teacher, and friend of many years.
- To TnT, you know who you are, thank you for standing by me.

Special Acknowledgments

- To Sue Hammond, David Cooperrider, Diana Whitney for the teachings of Appreciative Inquiry; they are the underpinnings for the Circle of Transformation.

"Our freedom extends only as far as our consciousness reaches.

Beyond that we succumb to the influences of our environment"[1]

— Carl Jung

Introduction

Soul-Searching: What Do You Really Want for Your Life?

"What do you really want for your life?"

What do you really want for your life? The energy of the power of '**YES**' always works to attract back to you that which you have sent forth as a dominant thought, want, or desire. The question is, "What are you actually sending forth as your dominant thought or desire?"

To find the answer to this question, and other 'right' questions, one must embark upon a journey; the journey of Self-discovery, a.k.a., Self-inquiry, Self-observation or Self-awareness. Self-discovery involves detecting and then shedding the "old beliefs" that no longer serve us in life. Through this unmasking and peeling process, we begin to realize that we are the person who is responsible for our life and who has the power to shift and shape the conditions of our life.

We come to understand that there is a powerful energy or power with in us and it desires to attract to us our highest good. However, we must learn how to consciously work with that power in order that our _highest good_ might be expressed. Revealing how to consciously engage with this Attractor Energy is the goal of *The Power of* '**YES**.'

'**YES**' works like a magnet as it attracts to us the Creative, Positive, Universal Energy – in accordance, of course – with <u>*our most dominant*</u> desire, thought, and word. As preparation for the journey into a deeper understanding of the workings of the Power of **'YES'**, please take a moment and reflect upon the following question: *"What do I really want for my life?"*

"What do I really want for my life?"

The Cosmic 2x4 Experience

"... the greater the tension, the greater the potential.
Great energy springs from a correspondingly great
tension of opposites."[2]

—Carl Jung

Throughout history humankind has utilized the venues of stories, chants, song, poems, odes, wall drawings, and more to share their legends, tales, practices, and traditions. Story—both oral and written—has been and continues to be a popular choice of expression for sharing ones experiences, customs and rituals. Why? Because, story gets people involved at a cellular level and has the capacity to touch a person on a deep feeling level. Narrative and written accounts that chronicle the journey through the mysterious passages of life serve to share the essence of who we are and what we have experienced, individually and collectively. Telling one's own personal story, sharing the personal parts of ones life is seen as an authentic action (AA). It is with this intention, that I share my story with you.

Not long ago I found myself in the midst of an unexpected experience. It began when the universe clobbered me over the head with the proverbial Cosmic 2x4, it happened both, literally and figuratively.

One evening while I was participating in a retreat program at work, I slipped and fell. My head – meeting the arm of a wooden chair – broke my fall. The diagnosis was mild traumatic brain injury. During the four month period that followed, I lost much of my short-term memory. Ultimately, in order to engage properly in the healing process, I had to take a leave of absence from my place of employment and service in ministry.

This was a difficult and tumultuous time for me. Initially, everything was new and everything was strange. It was a paradox. Not going to work was difficult. I had worked continuously for nearly 40 years, without ever taking much more than three weeks off at any given time. The loss of memory was frustrating; in addition it made me mad. I felt sorry for myself and I felt a little frightened.

After about two weeks of engaging in this self-destructive behavior, I had an epiphany during meditation. I "saw" myself. I saw how I was acting and how I was reacting to what was happening to me. All the chaos, frustration, weariness, concern, and madness that I was exhibiting, was revealed through short clips of pictures in my mind's eye. I gasped. I felt horrified that I would behave like this. After all didn't I know better than this? Hadn't I learned more than this? Wasn't I capable of facing life's slings and arrows?

After a few moments of partaking in this monkey mind chatter, I realized what I was doing. With this type of questioning I was heaping guilt, shame, and blame upon myself – along with the help of the three sisters – shoulda, coulda, woulda. So, I chose to stop, take a deep breath, look at my reactive behaviors and to review how they were affecting my life and healing process.

I chose to stop asking, "Why did this happen to me?" I began to think of 'right' questions, questions that would move me into a new frame of reference. In making this choice, I knew that I was being invited to step into the unknown and trust that whatever I needed would be there to support me. I have named this time of trusting the Unknown; 'dancing at the edge of mystery.'

After this, I began to ask myself the same questions that I pose to you throughout this book. "What do I really want for my life?" "How can I make this a positive experience?" "What can I do that would be productive?" "What do I want to draw more of into my life?" What can I let go of?

The universe had dealt me a hand and now it was time for me choose how I wanted to play it. If I was going to say, '**YES**', to greater possibility revealing itself, then I had to change my attitude and behaviors. When in meditaton I asked the question, "What do I really want for my life?" The answer I received was somewhat strange. I realized that I wanted a healing, but I wanted a healing that would be an upliftment for my soul and move me towards a greater awareness of spiritual growth and maturity.

I realized that in order for this to happen I would have to surrender all of my expectations, all of my frustrations, and make room for the possibility of something *greater* to emerge. In my heart I knew that what was being asked of me was that I be willing to surrender all my thoughts and wants and move into a state of peace about everything that was happening. Up to now, my concern about my memory not coming back was causing me great frustration, not peace. I realized that I was being asked to "dance at the edge of mystery" and await the unfolding of the lesson of the experience.

The edge of mystery, I find, is an interesting place to sit, be still, and contemplate life. The edge of mystery is the border's edge of ' the next movement.' It is a place where the 'stirrings' begin to bubble, where we must 'sit' for awhile and allow the questions to be formed and the answers to ripen. Through consciously permitting all of these facets of growth entrance to our awareness we are led into shifts in consciousness. these shifts ultimatley create changes in our lives, and transformation on all levels of our being.

Through consciously breathing in and breathing out, centering myself, staying calm, and being focused on the gift of the experience; I surrendered fully into the mystery of what this experience was desiring to teach me.

I said, *"YES! I will dance at the edge of mystery. I will allow the Unseen and the Unknown to work Itself through me."* So dance I did, sit I did, laugh I did, contemplate my navel I did, walk I did, read I did, rest I did, and prayer I did. BUT, I did not worry! I let that all go.

Within a very short time, the Creative force of the Great Unknown began to move through me. I started writing as if someone else was guiding my thoughts and hands. What came through me, I call, **Soul Searching's**. These are odes and poems came that reflect the struggles, fears, hopes, joys, and understandings that I gleaned during this transformation and healing process. (See Epilogue for odes and poems.)

What I did not realize, immediately, was that each time I wrote I was sending a healing message throughout my cellular structure. As each ode and poem revealed itself, simultaneously, there was a peeling away of another layer of unconscious muck and mire – old stuff that had been running my life for years. As the writings turned into a collection, I realized that they were part of my healing process. So, heal I did! **'YES'**! **'YES'**! **'YES'**!

When I look back on the situation, I now know that I had many choices and many routes that I could have taken, but I had to make the choice as to the one that I wanted. Choice was the key and intention was the key hole that my choices had to fit into, perfectly, or they would not work.

I created an intention to live life with a sense of spaciousness, grace and ease, so the choices I made had to be congruent with that decision. Taking everything into consideration, I chose to retire from the traditional grind of daily, organizational work and to continue with my healing process. The choices that I was making were going to take me to the edge of mystery, again. Those choices continue to be right, for this moment; I am at peace, living in joy and all my needs are being met.

What evolved out of that cosmic 2x4 experience was a deep understanding of the power of '**YES**' as an attractor for the creative, positive, Universal Energy. It is that understanding that led to the odes and poems, to the concepts of the *Power of 'YES,'* and the innovation of the *Circle of Transformation.*

Yes, change happens in life; however the key is to always be 'consciously' prepared to say '**YES**' to life, to change, to stirrings, to forward movement, transformation, _S_elf-discovery, and to dancing at the edge of mystery. The *Circle of Transformation* (see diagram at end of chapter) is a teaching model that symbolizes the movements we experience as we traverse through the process of _S_elf-discovery and transformation. It is a representation of the ever-circular, upward, evolving spiral of spiritual and personal maturity.

The *Circle of Transformation* incorporates the symbology of a circle to represent the continuity and continuation of all ideas and of life. Creating the concept of a circle with arrows that appear to be moving in a clockwise direction. They represent specific fundamental patterns of thought and behavioral movements that occur during times of change and transition. The arrows also symbolize the movement of a positive core life-giving energy that runs through each person. In the center of the circle is a Center-Point which is home to our Higher Power and the positive life-giving energy. That Energy flows forth continually and freely to 'nourish' all facets of our growth and becomes fully potent when we say, "YES".

The ultimate intention for the use of the tools and techniques shared in *the Power of 'YES'* and *the Circle of Transformation* is to evolve spiritual and personal maturity. As was stated, *the Circle of Transformation* represents specific fundamental patterns of thought and behaviors which are required for forward movement during times of change and transition. Together, the movements around the circle represent a blueprint for personal and collective growth and empowerment. The concepts of *the Circle of Transformation* are in harmony with the teachings of Universal Truth and the Appreciative Inquiry Model.

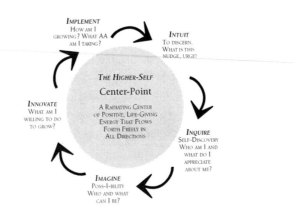

The Circle of Transformation:
Intuit, Inquire, Imagine, Innovate, Implement

> "Whether you think you can
> or think you can't, you are right!"
> —Henry Ford

Intuit:

Intuit is defined as: *"To know something instinctively, instinctive belief, without actual evidence, immediate knowledge."*[3] In the stage of Intuit we are about the work of discerning what it is that we are feeling or experiencing. We discern that something internally, is nudging us. We feel a discontent; have a dream of more for our life; or, sense a desire to do something different. We may not be aware of exactly what 'wants' to express, but we feel its interior movement. We begin to 'look and see,' by asking questions that will open the way for something new to reveal itself.

Consciously, or unconsciously, we are using our power of intuition to intuit what it is that is desiring to move through us. As we are open to this 'looking' within process, we are saying **'YES'** to a greater movement of positive life-energy moving through us. What the nudge we are feeling is working to do is to let us know that we are ready for a change in our life. Our work is to discern the movement and then be willing to engage with it, in a journey to wholeness. The question is, *"Will we say,* **'YES?'**

Inquire:

The Inquire or Self-Inquiry phase engages us in the process of deeper exploration into what wants to shift or change; this examination has the capacity to lead us into permanent change and transformation. However, in order to transform one must discover what it is that desires to shift and/or grow. This is accomplished through inquiring and delving into our past experiences in a positive manner and fashion. In doing this we open the way to uncover old worn-out beliefs and replace them with new awareness' that will create a brighter future.

When we inquire we use language such as, "tell me about what worked? What was/is meaningful to you? What have I done right in similar situatons? What can make this a win/win?" We use questions that are grounded in affirmation and appreciation; inquiry is accomplished through learning the art of asking the 'right' question.

When we ask the right questions, we are actually strengthening our ability to perceive new ideas and possibilities. As we utilize right questioning as a personal practice we are reinforcing the potential for positive outcome. We are inquiring as to what is right and good about us or the group we are involved with – and not trying to find out how bad we have been or who can we blame for our issues.

Imagine:

Imagine is defined as; *a form or image in mind, to see or hear something unreal.*[4] Thus, we create new images in our minds eye which begin to shift our perspective about who we are and what we can do.

Imagine, Imagine, Imagine! Can you imagine where you will be five years from now? What about ten years from now? Imagining is about vision and envisioning the future. Can you imagine being a positive, energetic person? Imagining remembers the best of what has been and invites us to amplify that. It opens us to possibility and gives us the insight to invite those that can help fulfill and/or stimulate creativity around our vision.

Who do you dare to be? How big do you dare to 'play?' How big is the container for your imagination? Does playing small serve you or anyone you are associated with? Once you start to get a feel for your true nature, potential, and possibility you can never return to playing small. The opposite of playing small could be considered as playing 'big.' Playing big, however, is not referring to the ego or acting like a big shot; it is referring to a sense of generosity of spirit and intention. A truly 'big' person, like a Mother Theresa has a sense of humility and wholeness about them, and understands their self-worth and value.

Mother Theresa said, *"We cannot all do great things, but we can all do small things greatly!"* What if everything we thought, every action we took was dedicated to doing small things greatly? Eventually, small things done over and over with joy, conviction, intention, and a sense of great passion, can add up to great things for our lives.

Dare to imagine your future, your finances, your health, your relationships, your perfect place of service in the world – dare to imagine and dream big! Open the flood gates of creativity and let it flow through you as you create scenarios of greater good for your life and those around you.

Did you know that change begins the moment you dare to ask the bigger question? Dare to ask your deepest questions; for it is said that the more positive the question, the greater and longer-lasting will be the change in your life. You know where you have been and what you have been doing – are you ready to imagine and experience something new?

Innovate:

Albert Einstein said, *"What would the universe look like if I were riding on the end of a light beam at the speed of light?"* How innovative can you be? To innovate means to *"try out new ideas."* Are you willing to try new ideas? Are you willing to learn how to design your perfect universe through the power of your thoughts? Are you willing to give form to new values and ideas? Once you have imagined possibility, are you willing to innovative new avenues of authentic action.

What does authentic action look like? Authentic action always ends in an implementation of a fresh new idea, a shift in awareness, or a change of behavior and attitude. Quoting Albert Einstein again, we get a feel for how change happens; *"No problem can be solved from the same level of consciousness that created it. We must learn to see the world anew."* So, dare to be innovative. Design a new idea, or a fresh authentic action.

You know where you have been, it is where you are going that you want to shape. What do you want to create, re-create, or change? Are you ready for a new set of beliefs, a personal or culture change, a relationship change, or ...?

When engaging with innovation it helps to think about a time when you experienced a positive flow of energy and power moving through a particular situation or experience that you were involved with. What did that positive energy feel like? What created the flow of energy? How did you participate? What were you doing? What knowledge did it leave you with? How can you innovate or recreate an outcome that is similar? When you ask these types of questions you are engaging in asking, 'right' questions.

Implement:

To implent is defined as: *"... a requirement for something needed in order to achieve something else, to carry out – as in taking authentic action – to put something in effect, to provide somebody with the tools or other means to do something."* [5]

Although, it appears that the circle has a starting point – Intuit – and an ending point – Implement – the circle is never-ending. As soon as we complete one round of growth on the circle we are ready to start another – if we are willing to participate. Also, often, the the phases of the circle overlap. We continue to grow and expand in awareness, as long as we are willing to consciously engage.

Einstein also said, *"There are only two ways to live your life. One is as though nothing is a miracle. The other is as though everything is a miracle."* Eric Butterworth in his book *Spiritual Economics* shares, *"You can live your life from a consciousness of 'No', or 'YES and WOW.'"* It is your choice, as to what will you implement in your life.

Planned steps get us to where we want to be in the

next moment, and the next week, next month, next year. Remember, positive thoughts and authentic actions generate more positive thoughts and authentic actions.

Goethe says, *"If you can dream it, you can achieve it?"* So use your intuitions, inquiries, imaginations, and innovations to create a vision and then, dare to implement that vision. Find a spark and flame it into a blazing fire of authentic action – action that will change your life, if you dare!

Right now everything is a possibility, but possibility becomes reality when carried forth with intention, conviction and passion. Go for it!

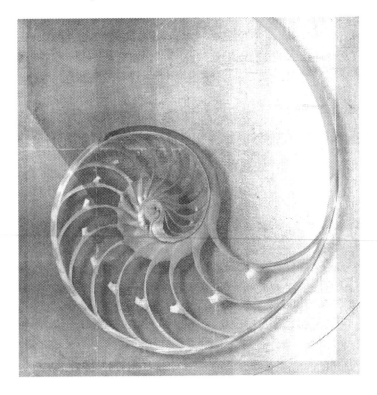

A 'YES' Experience: *The Circle of Transformation*

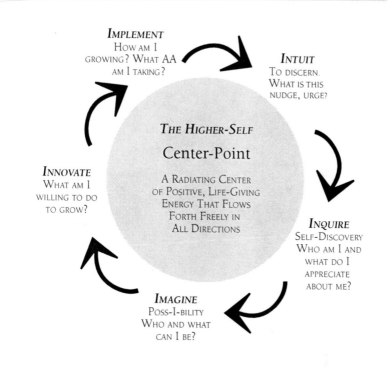

IMPLEMENT
How am I
growing? What AA
am I taking?

INTUIT
To discern.
What is this
nudge, urge?

THE HIGHER-SELF
Center-Point

A Radiating Center
of Positive, Life-Giving
Energy That Flows
Forth Freely in
All Directions

INNOVATE
What am I
willing to do
to grow?

INQUIRE
Self-Discovery
Who am I and
what do I
appreciate
about me?

IMAGINE
Poss-I-bility
Who and what
can I be?

The arrows symbolize the positive core life-giving energy in motion. The circle is the gestalt of the entire process; the potential of the living energy of 'YES.' At the Intuit phase of the circle, the person is often unaware of that which is desiring to emerge. By the time the person moves around the circle to the Implement phase they have opened themselves to new awareness' and have transformed on some level of Being. The circle overlays a spiral, which contnually moves one upward and suggests interconnecton and interplay of the phases. The circle is also never-ending for as soon as we complete one round on the spiral/circle is we are invited to start another. Thus, we continue to grow and expand, as long as we are willing to consciously engage.

"A journey of a
thousand miles
begins with the
first step."

— Lao-Tzu

Chapter 1
The Circle of 'Transformation': Intuit

"Are You Listening?"

Change – Why Would I Want to do That?

In each person, group, or organization there is a, "... *'positive change core'—and it assumes that every living system has many untapped and rich and inspiring accounts of the positive. Link the energy of this core directly to any change agenda and changes never thought possible are suddenly and democratically mobilized.* " [6]

"*The traditional approach to change is to look for the problem, do a diagnosis, and find a solution. The primary focus is on what is wrong or broken; since we look for problems, we find them. By paying attention to problems, we emphasize and amplify them. ...[so] we look for what works... The tangible result of the inquiry process is a series of statements that describe where the [person] wants to be, based on the high moments of where they have been. Because the statements are grounded in real experience and history, people know how to repeat their success*" [7]

As stated earlier, the Circle of Transformation, is a sister model to Appreciative Inquiry; which, "... *focuses us on the positive aspects of our lives and leverages them to correct the negative. It's the opposite of 'problem-solving.*" [8]

To uncover these positive aspects of life we utilize, "... *the art and practice of asking questions that strengthen a system's capacity to heighten positive potential. It mobilizes inquiry through crafting an 'unconditional positive question...*'"[9]

The Power of '*YES*' asserts that '**YES**' is the positive-core life energy inherent in each person and/or organization. '**YES**' as an energy works on a persons behalf in the grander scheme of things; '**YES**,' as a living-energy, desires to express and expand itself through its vehicle of expression -- always.

Engagement of the Power of '**YES**' is facilitated by intuiting that something is desiring to shift; making a conscious acknowledgment of the presence of the positive-core '**YES**' energy; then asking positive ('right') questions. Through these activities we are lead to deeper levels of self-awareness, new potentials, and possibilities.

The Historical –Psychological Problem Solving Process	The Power of 'YES,' A.I., & Universal Truth Principles Positive-Solution Oriented Process
Core Theory:	Core Theory:
We have a problem (person or situation) which needs to be resolved.	We have a mystery, let us embrace the person or situation and discover what is desiring to be birthed.
We ask about and look for all the problems and issues	We ask what is working now & what worked in the past?
We begin to label the problems and/or persons	We look for resolutions and answers that already exist
We focus on limitations and lack	We focus on the positive and that which will create energy
We work to fix what's out of order or in disarray	We increase & strengthen what is already working & positive
We find out who is to blame	We see who we can affirm
We learn from errors, fault-finding, and inadequacies	We learn from that which works or is good

Adapted from a work by Steve Lanktin

A 'YES' Experience: Igniting the Spark

As you participate in this experience, stay open to possibility. Answer the questions without any concern about not being seen as humble, for in this moment you are playing really 'big.'

Think about a time when you experienced a positive flow of energy and power moving through you and a particular experience that you were involved with?

What did that positive energy feel like?

What created the flow of energy?

How did you participate, what were you doing?

What knowledge did it leave you with?

How can you recreate a similar outcome?

What is the spark that you can identify, that you can flame into a blazing fire of authentic action? e.g. "I was on a team where I was given support to create my own project. This support helped me believe in myself."

Spark: When I am supported and validated I express myself easily.

YES!

Do you recall the shampoo commercial in which a woman was in the shower, having an organic experience, washing her hair? Do you remember what the words were that she was using to express the depths of the intensity of the moment? She was ecstatically repeating, "YES!" "YES!" "YES!"

While we watched that commercial we could feel the intensity of her experience. Her resounding 'YES' had an effect on us, as the listener. Whether we wanted to buy the shampoo or not, was secondary to the feeling that we walked away with. We knew she was completely involved in her experience. It left no doubt. She was involved in washing her hair and she was enjoying the experience. What if we could hold that intensity of intention, with the ideas that we desired to manifest?

Personally, I have a love affair with the word, 'YES.'I have always felt that the word 'YES' has a cosmic meaning that we, as a species, not yet fully understood. 'YES' is a verb that connotes action in motion; for a verb is defined as, "*a word used to show that an action is taking place, or to indicate the existence of a state or condition*" [10]

In my book, *The Spiritual Intrapreneur*, there is a definition for the word 'YES' given in the form of an acronym: "Y.E.S." stands for:

Your Empowerment System

'YES' acts an empowering agent for good when one speaks the word aloud or silently, combined with an intensity of feeling. For what happens is that when

'**YES**' is shared in this manner, it is recognized by the Universe as an approval, an endorsement that is sent forth into the universal Substance or Energy and acts as a magnet of attraction.

This magnet of attraction draws back to us that which we have set forth as our desire combined with our intention. Thus through the activity of the spoken "**YES**," we open the way for the universe to bring us that which we yearn for in our life.

'**YES**,' is a creative energy that lives within each one of us and is waiting to be released from its imprisonment; for '**YES**' desires to go forth and co-create our highest good in conjunction with us. However, to do this we must take an active part in this co-creative activity.

How do we do this? It is so simple, and yet, profound. We only have to be willing. We must be willing to take authentic action. To speak our '**YES**' into the universe with conviction, (like the woman in the shower shampooing her hair) while holding an intensity of feeling and belief that what we say will come to pass.

The simple act of being willing to step up and take authentic action, while holding both a conviction, belief, and an intention about what we are sending forth creates sends forth a stream of energy that imprints upon the invisible, universal Energy and Substance. This Substance is all around us and holds within It the power to change and transform the conditions of our life. It awaits our willingness to participate through our '**YES**.'

'**YES**' is a statement of faith that says, "I know I can do this." "I know this can happen." "I know that I can realize my dream." "I am somebody." "I have skills." "I am worthy."

One reason I respect the word '**YES**' so much is that 'YES' is tied to the beginning of everything. For in the beginning something had to say, "**YES.**" Whether it was a Divine Being saying '**YES**' to the creation of Being; or, just simply our parents consenting to be at the same place in the same moment. Something, some Universal Energy said '**YES**,' to a co-creative experience happening in that moment. A '**YES**' or consent was sent out into the Universal Substance and the Substance responded – that is how it works.

When we become aware that there is a greater Power that lives within us and that Its Energy desires to co-create with us as a blazing, radiant, passionate, intense fervor and potency – why would we not be willing to participate with It? '**YES**', as a co-creative partner, only comes to the forefront of our awareness when:

- We accept that there is a potential within us that is waiting to be drawn forth.
- We begin to move forward by taking responsibility for our lives and the conditions of our of life.
- When we are willing to engage with It.

Be aware that engaging with the co-creative '**YES**' will ultimately tear asunder the veils of illusion and negative beliefs that we hold about ourselves, our lives, and others in our life.

A 'YES' Experience: An Extraordinary Being

Think of someone you admire, greatly – they can be living or not. What is it that you admire about them? What makes them extraordinary in your eyes? Consider all of the traits, characteristics, and behaviors that you admire and makes this person special to you. What are your top three items? Do this before you read on, please.

_____

Look again at the list. Are you aware that you could not see these ideals, behaviors, traits and characteristics in this other person, if they did not exist with in you? You just couldn't see them if they were not a part of who you are. With this in mind, look at the traits again and now consider how you express them. Be fair and kind to your self and look deeply at who you really are. Please, take time, to journal your thoughts and responses from this exercise.

_____

_____

_____

_____

_____

_____

_____

_____

'YES', an Affirmation

"People should not consider so much what they are
to do, as what they are."
— Meister Eckhart

'YES' depending upon how we use it, is a statement of faith and an affirmation that says, "I can do this." "I know this can happen." "I know I can realize my dream." "I am somebody." "I have skills." "I am worthy." We might ask, "If **'YES'** is so powerful, then why doesn't it work each time I ask for something? This question has many answers, which include, but are not limited to:

- We do not know what we really want.

  –We say we do, but we really don't, for when asked what we want we say, "I don't care. It doesn't matter, you pick."

- We often say **'YES'** and **'No'** at the same time.

  –We say, **'YES,'** then immediately negate our **'YES,'** with a **BUT,** a **MAYBE,** a **PERHAPS** it will work, **I THINK**, etc."

–Our words have power; they are connected to our thoughts which create our intention.

- We are not willing to take responsibility for shifting our thoughts into a direction that will take us into a higher level of interaction and that will facilitate bringing us our highest good.

  –We allow our thoughts to run rampant and unchecked. We do not take charge and stop all the chatter, worry, and anxiety – which also negates our **'YES.'**

- We say one thing and do another.

  –This is called being incongruent. The universe supplies our needs according to our clarity, purpose, intention, and focus. You will get what you ask for – that is the LAW.

- We play the victim.

  –Playing the victim allows us to blame others for our problems; making them responsible for our misery, grief, sadness, problems, lack of joy, and so on.

Playing a victim – "Not me," you say! I would ask you – how often have you blamed your boss, your spouse, your partner, the kids, your parents, your lack of education, bad timing, etc., for your woes? (We will discuss this further in another chapter.) "What do you really want?" is not a rhetorical question? It is asked in order that we may stop and think about what is important to us and what we really want for and in our life. If we do not know what we truly want, how can the Universe give it to us? If we do know what we want, how can we get the Universe to bring it to us? Be careful of your thoughts and words for they are always affirming what you want. Be sure that your thoughts are clear and that your words are spoken with clarity and that you are affirming what you want and not what you don't want. Your words have power and can determine the fate of what you are asking for? So, choose your words wisely and consciously.

Did you know that when you use the following words as a **'YES'** answer to a question being asked of you – you are in actuality saying, **'NO'**. These **'NO,'** words include but are not limited to; perhaps, could be, might, yep, uhmmm, I'll try, let's see what happens ... From a universal, cosmic standpoint – 'YES' is 'YES' and anything else is a, 'NO.' I would invite you, for the next 48 hours to be observant of your words. What are the words that you use to say, 'YES?' Think about this question, it is a 'right question, for delving deeper into your discovery process.

Dancing at the Edge of Mystery

At a workshop that we were co-facilitating in Nashville, Tennessee, my dear friend Andrew Harvey, shared a story about a petroglyph, a rock drawing, that he had seen in the desert. This rock drawing touched his soul and spoke to his heart. The following is my summation of what he shared about the drawing and our combined thoughts on its relationship to the energetic 'YES' of the universe:

The gift of the rock drawing was left by the indigenous people, known as the Anasazi's. It is an ancient picture drawn on a vast, molten copper-colored rock. The drawing depicts two stick figures, a man and a woman, dancing with their arms outstretched above their head. This man and woman positioned in a dance of praise and affirmation are so consumed by the sacred Energy of the Universe that Its Power expressed as lightning, flashes from the soles of their feet wildly in all directions. These lightning flashes are streaming out as chaotic bursts of electrified Light-Energy that cannot be contained.

It would appear that these two are dancing to the rhythm of the **'YES'** of life. That this sacred Energy of **'YES'** lives within them and has been re-kindled as a surging and pulsating passion that moves throughout every cell of their being. In this dazzling reflection of the co-creative power of the universal **'YES,'** this blazing stream of Energy pours forth from them as fire flashing out through the cellular structure of their bodies.

With one gesture of "YES," these two beings are offering themselves to God, wholly and completely. **'YES'** possesses them and that same **'YES'** transfigures them into a state of Oneness with the Source of sacred Power. Offering themselves to their God, they dance at the edge of mystery and in a state of Divine bliss. Dancing with un-abandoned pleasure, they know not where their dance will lead them. They only know that dance they must and dance they do; dancing with a grand gesture of 'YES,' they open their whole self to being filled by an energy greater than themselves.

They are dancing at the edge of mystery, for **'YES'** calls them to the dance at this edge and compels them to give themselves as an offering to the One. This act of surrender sends forth a powerful, but silent, energetic vibration into the universal Substance. This silent resonance co-creates a mighty force of glory and fuses them in oneness with the One. And although the picture reveals that their sacred posture of surrender invites the energy of the creative **'YES'** into their midst, it also reveals that their posture is one of total freedom. Part of the mystery is the dance of surrender and the dance of freedom taking place in the same moment.

The surrender is not an act of sacrifice; on the contrary, inherent in the surrender ones feels that it is an act of freedom that opens their hearts to a direct transmission of Love. A person looking on can see with the naked eye, how their '**YES**' is creating a joining of body, heart, spirit and soul into the Oneness of Being. A coming together of Source and Power, mind and heart, light and dark, body and soul, spirit and matter, surrender and freedom, and masculine and feminine – in what could be construed as a cosmic orgasm of the universe.

'**YES**' lives in the depths of your being and longs to unite you with the One Presence. Have you experienced that '**YES**' in your life? If you have, think about a time when you released this inner splendor and you knew it? What were you doing and who else was involved? How did it make you feel?

If you have not had the experience of '**YES**' coursing through out your being, do you desire to release this inner splendor, this creative activity of '**YES**' and have it work consciously in your life? Here is an exercise that can help to ignite the sacred fire.

A 'YES' Experience: Dancing at the Edge of Mystery

I invite you to take a moment, in the privacy of your home, in the woods, at the waters edge or wherever it may be that you choose, to stand and stretch out your arms in a conscious offering to the '**YES**' of your being. Stretch forth your arms and like the Anasazi couple be willing to dance at the edge of mystery; inviting both surrender and freedom to enter in.

Stand not as a victim with the burdens of life weighing you down, but stand-up straight, with your arms outstretched, in the universal pattern of '**YES**.' Stand as a one willing to participate in the Divine dance of Life. Stretch forth your arms over your head and BE the living body prayer of the universal '**YES**' as you create the letter Y.

Now, begin to speak your '**YES**' into the universal Substance. Speak your '**YES**' with Power, with conviction and with an intention that reveals that you are willing to dance at the edge of mystery – come what may!

What is it that you want to say '**YES**' to? What does your heart desire more than anything else? Even if you do not know, just be willing to surrender into the mystery desiring to make itself known through you.

Speak your '**YES**' loudly into the forming Substance of the universe; speak your '**YES**' over and over and over and over and over – do not be self-conscious, just BE willing. The universal substance is waiting to respond to the vibration and power of the movement of your spoken word throughout its living body of energy.

Speak your "**YES**," 20 or 30 or 40 or 100 times. Feel It's Power as it moves throughout your mind, body and soul. Let the '**YES**' consume you.

Surrender into Its Energy, release and let go, be drawn into Its Vibration. Allow the universal '**YES**' to begin to resonant within your being. You will know when you have surrendered into freedom. You will feel when you have let yourself be released into the One, be not afraid for Absolute Love will never harm you.

Once you are complete, when you have finished

speaking '**YES**' for the desires of <u>self-transformation and growth</u>, now, dedicate '**YES**' to the calling forth of a project of service for the universe; a project that you would like to consciously and actively be a part of.

You may choose to dedicate your '**YES**' to the upliftment of global consciousness; to the elimination of abuse towards children, women, and/or animals; to awakening the consciousness of humankind to Divine Love; to World Peace, to finding a cure for a disease or whatever it is that is moving in your heart in the moment.

This is the time for "**YES!**" Let us birth the '**YES**' of the Divine into the world, NOW!

In your journal, or on this page, write about your experience with the Cosmic "YES."

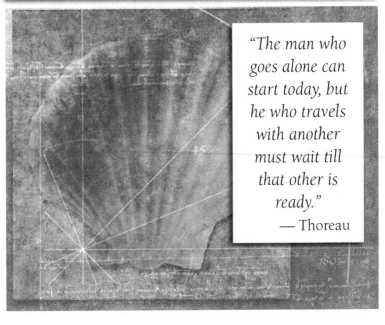

"*The man who goes alone can start today, but he who travels with another must wait till that other is ready.*"
— Thoreau

Chapter 2
The Circle of 'Transformation': Inquire

Self-Inquiry – A Journey Inward

Gear for the Journey

"What are you waiting for?
The journey into the Unknown begins
by saying **"YES!"**

—TGB

Anytime we go on a trip, we must take the correct clothes, toiletries, gear, shoes, etc. If we are going camping we probably would not take a suitcase full of dressy clothes. We pack appropriately for the experience.

As we consciously engage with the *Circle of Transformation,* there are tools, techniques, and aids that can help us on our journey to wholeness. Each tool is powerful in its self and yet, when combined with a few, or several of the others, they often create something akin to combustion; for they help to "blow" us open and make the journey a little "easier." If one of these tools speaks to your heart, begin now to inquire about its right usage and then put it into action. These tools include, but are not limited to the following:

Taking Authentic Action

Implementation of all authentic action is supplemented by utilizing the S.M.A.R.T. technique. S.M.A.R.T. holds the space for our actions to be authentic through being: Specific, Measurable, Achievable, Relative, and Time-specific. Actions for implementation that include these elements tend to move us from possibility to reality, quickly.

Self-Observation and Self-Honesty

Self-discovery, Self-observation, Self-awareness or, Self-inquiry with out practicing Self-honesty is futile. In fact, it is useless. Nothing will come of the exploration because when the person is not willing to look, see, and be honest about what is really going on, they will stay mired in defensiveness, control, and status quo. Excuses get us no where and only serve to keep us where we are.

Creating & Honoring Intention

Intention is what we intend to do, if we are engaging with the positive life-giving core energy we must intend to keep our words clear, our hearts open, and follow through on that which we say we will do.

Making Conscious Choices

Making conscious choices shifts our thinking and moves us toward knowing that we are responsible for our lives and not just victims of life. We make conscious choices when we are willing to look at what is happening, see it for the way it reality is, be honest about how we participated in creating this reality and then be willing to go another direction.

Prayer, Conscious Releasing & Letting Go, Forgiveness, and Presence Pauses/Breathing Techniques

The conscious practice of prayer, forgiveness, and releasing and letting go helps us to align with our Higher Power. During times of stress and stretch using the breath as calming influence is important to the overall outcome of any situation. By pausing to consciously engage with the breath we have the ability to move from reaction to response. Prayer and meditation has the ability to align our mind with a Higher Power. This is not about <u>talking</u> to a Higher Power and telling them what we want, real prayer, is about getting quiet and listening to what the Higher Power has to say to us.

Releasing and letting go happens when we surrender to the idea that there is a Higher Power that knows more than we do and we become willing to let It start working in our lives. Forgiveness is an authentic action that takes place as a result of praying and releasing. We start to realize that non-forgiveness hurts us more than it does the person we holding negative thoughts against. *"Forgiveness is the fragrance that Love sheds upon the heel of one who stepped on it."* [11](An adaptation of a quote by Robert Browning.)

Affirmations and Using Positive Self-Talk

Affirmations are a form of positive self-talk. Affirmations help to keep us centered, poised, and calm during stressful situations. Affirmations, affirm that which good and right and help to connect us a brighter future, now. *"I am calm, centered, and poised in mind and body, now."* Affirmations are short, clear, and concise and happen in the now moment. They are not a projection into the future.

Watching Your Internal Dialogue

The pitfalls of runaway internal mind chatter, a.k.a., Monkey Mind Chatter (MMC) are explained in Chapter 3: *Reality is not as Reality is ...* . When negative mind chatter is overcome, our thoughts become dominate forces for creating a better world to live in.

Knowing Reality is not as Reality is, Reality is as We Perceive It.

Life has only the meaning that we give to it. Think about this! We each create our reality according to our beliefs and past experiences.

What this means is that we use what has happened to us in the past to define what is happening to us now. Usually we project past thoughts and experiences onto what is happening, rather than seeing what is really occurring. Understanding the depth of what these statements mean can shift our perceptions and create a fresh perspective for our lives. It also helps us to step back and regroup in the midst of chaos. Asking positive life-giving questions has the capacity to help us reinvent our reality.

Engaging With Universal Laws and Principles

Laws and Principles are shared bodies of beliefs that do not change, they are eternal regardless of how we use or misuse them. Being universal Laws they work whether we like it or not. e.g., The Law of Attraction, you are the point in the universe where co-creation occurs. You will co-create according to the dominant thoughts and beliefs that you hold. If you are not happy with your life, learn how to change your thoughts and you can change your life.

Newton discovered the Law of Gravity, he didn't

invent it, it was always there; and so it is with us. We discover the Laws and then begin to practically apply them through our thoughts and actions.

In the book, *The Revealing Word*, by Charles Fillmore, we find the following written about Law:

"Laws of mind are just as exact and undeviating as the laws of mathematics. To recognize this is the starting point in finding [a Higher Power]. [We do] not make the law; the law is, and it was established for our benefit before the world was formed. Back of the judge is the law out of which s/he reads. Laws, whether natural or artificial, are but the evidence of an unseen power. The development of [humankind] is under law.

Creative mind is not only law, but is governed by the action of the law that it sets up ... a clear understanding of ourselves ... makes us realize that everything has its foundation in a rule of action, a law, that must be observed by both creator and created ... Divine law cannot be broken. It holds [us] responsible for the result of [our] labors ...

So in taking control of the forces within, keep on the affirmative side. Let the preponderance of your thought be positive, and do not spend much time saying, "I am not." You may find it helpful sometimes to say, "I am not afraid," but more often you should say, "I am bold, fearless, courageous." [12]

Laws and Principles are necessary for the realization of our true nature, as positive, energetic life-forces. There are many laws such as, the Law of Gravity discovered by Newton, but for this teaching we will focus on the Laws that underpin the true nature of our Being.

- The Law of Mind Action – The Law of Cause and Effect – The Law of Attraction

    –What you focus on expands. (This is a corollary Law to the Law of Expansion.)

– The thoughts you hold in mind will come to pass and be reflected in your life.

– Like attracts like.

– Where your attention goes energy flows.

– Law of Attraction—*"The law that all conditions and circumstances in affairs and body are attracted to us to accord with the thoughts we hold steadily in consciousness."* [13]

– All is in order because these Laws exist.

• The Law of Expansion

– *There is a "Substance or Energy [in the universe], although... undetectable—like yeast mixed into bread dough—is nonetheless, a powerful...catalyst that enables automatic expansion and growth in response to intention..."*

– *"...in response to[our]plans and intentions ... the tendency of things to expand in response to our thoughts can be useful, controllable, and can produce creations with real practical value ... things expand and grow in response to thought...*[14]

• The Law of Compensation – The Law of Giving and Receiving – The Golden Rule

– As you give so shall you receive or what goes round comes round.

• The Law of Non-Resistance

– That which you resist persists.

– That which you release in mind, cannot and will not hurt you.

- The Law of Forgiveness
  - As above, so below; the tendency for things to even out.
  - If we can be forgiven of our trespasses, we too must be willing to forgive others.
  - It is never too late to change; forgive and you will be forgiven.
  - Forgiveness changes you, not the other person.

Journaling:

Journaling is a staple of soul expression, and should be encouraged for both individual and group work. Journals are not shared, but remain a private experience that helps you to grow, transform, and get to know yourself better.

At first, the idea of keeping a journal may seem overwhelming or remind you of something you did when you were a teenager. We never outgrow the benefits of a personal journal, however. Journaling is a great tool for helping us chart our progress as we grow in life and in our business world. It allows us to remember in full detail, events that have shaped our personal and professional lives. Journaling provides you with a way to reflect upon your reactions, feelings, and thoughts to certain stimuli. It unfolds a road-map to your inner-self and a better understanding of how you react to different situations.

Taking Personal Inventories:

This includes writing down your thoughts, aspirations, goals, strong characteristics, and other things you want to remember about yourself. Often inventories such as the one here in the book, entitled, An Extraordinary Being, can reveal new and fresh insights about yourself. They may reveal that want to learn or improve a skill, overcome an old habit, modify a behavior, or that you are more creative than you have previously considered yourself to be.

Clearing Unfinished Business:

Perhaps there is someone in your professional or personal life with whom you would like to have a conversation, to clear up misunderstandings? However, you feel that having that conversation might create negative feelings. Use your journal as a mental and emotional clearinghouse. Once you see your thoughts on paper, many times the "charge" behind the emotional response becomes lessened and new ways to deal with the issues behind the reaction come to light. Thus, you can move forward in a positive way.

Watching for Patterns and Mile Markers:

After you have kept a journal for awhile, you will see patterns of behavior and events playing out throughout your life and career. This viewing of your life will help you honestly assess what is happening and why, and discover possibilities for improvement.

Observation of Rhythms:

Life contains periods of ebb and flow, ups and downs, highs and lows. Journaling allows you to observe your life rhythms.

Redefining Life:

By reviewing your recent or distant past, you can begin to reinterpret significant events and see them with new eyes.

Self Dialogue:

Journaling is a good way to ask yourself questions and then let the answers come from the center of your being rather than your rational or intellectual self. This opens opportunities for self-dialogue between you and your Higher Self, creating new insights into old problems and conditions, thus you get to know yourself and your world better.

Expressive Writing:

You say you can not write. I would beg to differ. If you know the alphabet and can use a pencil, you can write. The writing I am speaking about is not for publication but for your own self-observation. Write your thoughts down, keep track of your feelings, and check your responses vs. reactions through keeping a descriptive log.

Ask your Higher Self what your dreams meant last night and then listen and record the answers. This exercise is not difficult; it just takes a little training and a little discipline. As the years go by and you see in your own hand-writing, your history unfolded before you; it opens your mind and heart to new discoveries. I would also add, that writing can include the drawing of symbols or pictures, the creation of diagrams, or whatever helps you to remember and reveal.

A 'YES' Experience: What If?

Purpose: To encourage the sense of high self-esteem through Self-inquiry and Self-discovery. A sense of self-esteem that is based on realistic thoughts and not fantasy or pretend.

Materials: Pencil and paper or tape recorder and journal.

Setting: A quiet environment where one will not be disturbed.

A Glendale, California psychologist was reported to use this technique with very favorable results. It is a simple, yet powerful process of in-depth questioning that helps to uncover and discover a person's true feelings and motivations. (This also works with organizations that desire to find out answers to perplexing problems that keep nagging at their bottom line.)

As with any process of Self-discovery, the process only works as well as the depth of honesty behind it. The point of the exercise is to ferret out the true thoughts and/or feelings behind an issue or problem in the participant's life and to bring forth from the deepest levels of the unconscious a sense of resolution.

The directions are as follows;

1. Take an 8 1/2 x11 inch piece of paper and draw a circle with spokes, as shown. Create eight sections with the following headings -- physical, mental, emotional, spiritual, relational, business, finances, other (other is for you to decide how to label).

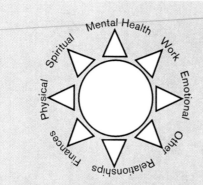

2. Take time to ponder each heading and the problems, issues, and growing edges of your life related to these sections. Write your thoughts/responses next to the corresponding section of the circle. Take several minutes to do this writing and reflecting.

3. Using the information that you have just written, select the one that is the most important to you.

4. Develop a question or statement for the item. It will be a fill-in-the-blank type question or statement.

> For instance, let us say that the priority that you selected was under the heading of physical health and the issue was of being tired all the time.

> You might develop a question or statement that looks like this;

> "I believe that I am tired all the time because
>
> _____ ."

5. Once you have your statement begin to speak it to your self, asking and listening for new answers. Provide not just one answer, but answer the ques-

tion over and over again with a different ending. Remember to make a mark * and/or comment by any answers that seem to elicit a feeling or response from you. Also, there is no right or wrong answer.

Example:

"I believe that I am tired all the time because

_____ ."

I don't get enough sleep.

I don't get enough sleep because I do not take my vitamins regularly.

I don't take my vitamins regularly because I forget or maybe I really don't think I am worthy of feeling good.
* Note: This answer brought tears to my eyes.

"I believe that I am tired all the time because

_____ ."

Because, I am not happy.

"I believe that I am tired all the time because

_____ ."

Because, I am not happy with my life.
* Note: Ah, this answer sent a chill down my spine.

6. Continue with this process until you feel that you have exhausted all your options or answers. This process is like peeling an onion. You are working to uncover what is at the core of your being. With each question you answer, you are peeling away a layer of "old stuff." With each layer that is peeled away you have better chance of getting to the truth of why you do what you do.

7. After you have finished review the *Notes to self and any other comments you have made. Look carefully at your answers and see if there is anything that keeps coming up or repeating itself.

   -Are there any common themes?

   -What seemed to move you?

   -Are there any common themes in your "aha's" or bodily responses?

   This exercise may or may not bring you an immediate insight, but don't let that fool you into thinking that nothing happened. Your answers may not come immediately, but they will stir and brew within you and you will begin to get a clear picture of yourself and the issue.

8. For each question that you get an insight to, begin to think about how you might start to create change for that situation. What might you implement as a new goal or, do as something creative to shift the energy around the situation?

The Art of Asking "Right" Questions

The rhythm of our life experiences has depth and dimensions. We can choose to live life from a frantic, hard-rock metal-like sound, moving us so fast that we hardly have time to catch our breath. Or, we can choose to live life from a rhythm that is so slow that it appears as if are we barely moving, accomplishing nothing. One of the goals of life is to learn to live from a rhythm that allows us to Be a place of balance, centered, poised, and peaceful.

The experiences and the appearances in our life ultimately come to teach us lessons; lessons about who we are, how we are showing up, how we are participating with the rhythm of life's energy and how that energy leaves us feeling after an experience. Do we feel empowered or disempowered; tired or exhilarated; happy or sad; chaotic or peace-filled?

To discover the lessons inherent in the experiences before us, often we need to engage in a process of honest questioning and self-dialogue, a.k.a., **S**elf-discovery. We can develop, with practice, what is known as the art of the questions. These types of questions glean positive, uplifting, imaginative responses from our past history and life experiences. This act of asking 'right' questions comes from the practice of inquiry.

In-quire' *(kwir), v., 1. the act of exploration and discovery. 2. To ask questions; to be open to seeing new potentials and possibilities. Synonyms: Discover, Search, and Systematic Exploration, Study."* [15]

The art of inquiry asks:

> "What possibilities exist that I have not thought about yet?"

> "What's the smallest change that could make the biggest impact on my life?"

> "What solutions would be a win/win/win?"

> "What makes my questions inspiring, energizing, and mobilizing?"

> "What have I done right in my life?"

> "How can I continue to build upon those "right" experiences?"

> "Am I ready to learn the lesson that life and it experiences is trying to reveal to me?"

> "Am I willing and ready to shift, change, and grow?"

> "Am I ready to wake-up and make conscious choices for my life?"

> "Am I engaging consciously in the experiences of my life?"

> "What thoughts can I shift or changes can I make in order for transformation to appear in the midst of this experience?"

When we consciously say, '**YES**' to the full expression of the lesson that our life experiences have to offer, we find that the universe rushes in to help us learn our lessons with as much ease and grace as possible. Why? Because we are not resisting the lessons anymore; we are consciously participating in them and with them.

The rhythm of life's experiences is always changing. Change is a constant in life. At times, the rhythm may be that of a march, requiring us to look straight ahead, stay on purpose, and persevere, not getting off course. At other times, the rhythm of change may swing us like a rhumba, wanting us to sway, swerve, and move in multiple directions quickly or perhaps, it may want us to not move at all. Occasionally, it may require that we be willing to move from the center of safety to the edge of mystery and tread into the fullness of the mystery's hidden, intense, dark, and rich space of Unknowing. The edge of mystery is the place where the real dance of life awaits us. Until we allow the rhythm of life's experiences to take us to the edge of mystery, we are only "playing" at being involved in life and in exploring the real issues of life.

Willingly moving to the edge of mystery moves us into a mind-set that honors the idea that we do not know everything and that we do not need to know everything – for we trust that there is something greater than we are that does know. Thus, the question becomes, "Will you say, '**YES**' to participating?"

A 'YES' Experience: Self-Awareness – Who Am I?

In this book or, in a journal answer this question to the best of your ability. Go to a quiet place, close your eyes and ask the following question over and over again. Each time something bubbles up, write it down – don't negate it or think that it is unimportant. Keep at this experience for a minimum of 5 minutes each.

Who am I? _____

Who am I? _____

Who am I? _____

Who am I? _____

Who am I? _____

What am I here to learn? _____

What am I here to learn? _____

What am I here to learn? _____

Is there something that I need to look at?

_____

Is there something that I need to look at?

_____

Is there something that I need to look at?

_____

Self-Inquiry: Who Am I?

The most important question
We can ask ourselves is; "Who am I?"
For the answer holds the secret to an empowered life.
                                            —TGB

Since the beginning of recorded history humanity has been bombarded with messages of lack, limitation and unworthiness. These messages have come through many channels, from organized religion to advertisements. We are told how we do not measure up. The subtle and not so subtle messages proclaim that we are not worthy because we are worms of the dust, we are bad, we are not smart enough, we are not thin enough, nor educated correctly, we can't do things right, etc. In fact, these are just a few of the messages that have been introduced into the collective psyche of humankind. As messages of this type are constantly repeated, they become ingrained in the consciousness (awareness) of humankind and act as an energetic force that holds us back from understanding who we are in our truest nature.

This lack of understanding around our true nature, acts as a wound that won't heal and has strength enough to run our lives. This wound has thwarted our spiritual and personal growth and evolution and has held us back, as a collective consciousness, from the full realization of our potential, and thus, from our true destiny. If humanity is going to continue to thrive we must begin now to create a new scenario for our future existence.

How do we create this new scenario for humankind?

By being willing to ask new questions and to say 'YES' to a new way of thinking and being in the world. Human beings are self-aware. We have the capacity to be conscious. However, most persons are not conscious of this capacity. They walk around asleep to the fact that there is something greater desiring to birth Itself through them. It takes a wake-up call to arouse within us the desire to be more self-aware. Even when we receive the wake-up call, often we go back to sleep-walking through life. To stay awake is not easy.

For the one who desires to **_consciously_** pursue _S_elf-awareness, the concept of being conscious holds within it certain ways of existing and acting. They include (but are not limited to):

* Observing how we act (_S_elf-observation)

* Asking questions that will spur growth

* Observing what we think

* Observing how we react to what we think

* Recognizing how we make decisions

* Recognizing how through the five senses of smelling, tasting, touching, hearing, and seeing we observe and experience our world and then realizing how this effects how we show-up on a day to day basis.

* Knowing what tools are available and making use of them

Our **_depth_** of _S_elf-awareness stems from the beliefs that we hold about whom we say we are. _S_elf-awareness is the underpinning of the spiritual journey. Please recognize that there is both self-awareness and _S_elf-awareness. To be self-aware, is to know that you exist and have certain capabilities that make you different from animal kingdom and from other people.

To be **S**elf-aware, holds within it the willingness to BE and to BE open to trusting that something **S**acred lives within. In this space of Being open and willing, we begin to "see" how frenetic our life has been. We begin to be aware of how we are assaulted by the chaos and cacophony of sounds and dis-chords that we call our life experience and how we have participated in it through our reactions to all of it.

When we are **S**elf-aware, we touch a place in our heart (or consciousness) that allows us to hear a new sound arising. The sound often arises as a question that comes from the interior of our being and asks, *"Is this all there is to life?"* It is a reverberation that comes from the heart's desire to find a new way of being in life.

Ultimately, through asking the question – *"Is this all there is?"* – we will be lead to a moment when we ask the eternal question. "Who am I?" "Who am I?" As I live my daily existence, who am I really, and is who I am now, who I want to be for the duration of this lifetime?"

Among all the questions one could ask themselves – "Who am I?" – is the most important one. Who am I as a mother or a father, a sister or a brother, a co-worker, or a citizen of the universe? In every role that life has given to us we begin to ask; who am I and how am I showing up?

By being willing to ask these questions, we begin to trample the illusions and rend the veils of ignorance of who we think we are in order that we might find out who we really are. We open an inner door, previously hidden, that when once opened, leads us to find the true essence of our life's meaning.

A 'YES' Experience: Who Am I? -- Meditation

Purpose: To center oneself in the midst of a chaotic day, or for inspiration, empowerment or clearing. (I used this meditation as part of my personal healing work when I had the head injury).

Setting: Individual inner-work that can be done at home, or in a group with a facilitator.

Materials: Chair, soft background music, candles and journal (optional).

Meditation:

I ask myself: "Who am I?" "What am I?"

In desiring to answer these questions I close my eyes and in order to find the answer as to where I exist within my body.

I bring my attention to my feet and ask: "Am I here in my feet?"

No! I do not exist in my feet.

If I lost my feet I would still exist? YES!

I move up my body still desiring to find who I am and where I exist.

I bring my attention to my knees, am I there? No, I do not exist in my knees. For if I lost my knees, I would still exist.

I bring my attention to my stomach, my chest, my head, my organ of the heart – do I exist there, in those places?

No! Then where do I exist?

I search myself from toenails to the topmost of my head and I cannot find me.

I ponder and ponder, "What is this mystery of my true identity?

Why is it that I have always thought I was either of this body or in this body?

Now I perceive that I am not of this body and I never was of this body.

I never could be totally encompassed in a body.

For "I," the "I" am that 'I' really am cannot be confined to a body.

As Moses saw the burning bush and heard the Voice, so I too hear the proclamation in every cell of my being – " I am that "I" Am.

The paradox is that I exist not within my body, and yet 'I' exist in every cell of my body.

Now I realize that it is not me that is looking out at me in the mirror. It is the 'I' which is looking out at me – the Invisible "I."

I cannot see It with my eyes, but I know that It is there.

I, me, the person the world calls _____ (insert your name).

Who do people say I am?

What are the labels that people (and myself) have placed on me?

It has been said that I am a mother/father, sister/brother, friend/no-friend, big-deal/no-deal, spiritual, rebel-rouser, blah, blah, blah.

What I know is that none of these labels are really the truth about who I am, for no one has ever seen the Real me for "I" am Invisible.

The persons that surround me have only seen their concept of who they think I am.

The real "Me" has not been seen, for "I" is everywhere and no where.

In quiet contemplation I know that the Invisible "I" is who I truly am.

When I know who "I" Am, I know who you are and what else is there to know?

A 'YES' Experience: One Desire

If you could take all the desires you have right now and put them into one desire, what would that desire look like? Keep your responses short and succinct. Please write your answer on this page, or in a journal that you will keep.

For the next seven days ask and then answer this question, then record your answer. At the end of seven days review all your statements and review for the following:

How are they the same? How do they differ?

What, if anything, is significant to you?

The Question: "If I could take all the desires I have right now and put them into one desire, what is that desire?"

Self-Knowledge

"Be willing to turn your wounds into wisdom"
—Oprah

Answering the question, "Who am I?" helps us to discover the real reason for our journey on this planet. Many centuries ago the Oracle of Delphi stated that in order to have wisdom one needed to *"Know Thyself."* Knowing thyself can be summed or understood more easily, through the words of a modern day mystic. "What you do speaks so loud I can't hear what you say." When we are not conscious, we say one thing and do another and often do not realize or do not care that this is how we are showing up. When we are conscious, we start to look at what we are doing and make sure that the doing and saying are in alignment.

Much of society in our country has come to equate ultimate happiness with success, power and control. If we are to be bigger, better and more successful at whatever we do, then we must have more power and more control. We begin to live by a "success at any cost" attitude and we allow this to be the guiding principle of our life.

When we live from the unconscious mode of, "success at any cost" mind-set, what we find is that there are negative attitudes and/or behaviors that we get seduced into using or participating in. These include, but are not limited to, some form of the following; manipulation, fear, greed, envy, jealousy, control, anger, lust, hatred, right at any cost, belittling others, segregation, , character assignation, "better than," making others wrong, and so forth. We use these attitudes and behaviors to further our mental invention of power and success. However, this unstable attitudinal house of cards can all too easily tumble down and one day we find that we have just gotten whacked with a life-shattering experience such as getting fired, losing a loved one, facing a sudden financial set-back, a severe health challenge, etc. The upset knocks us to our knees. We're left staring at the essential questions of "What is my life about?" and "Who am I?"

But our old illusions, attitudes and values cannot provide answers. We have just gotten a cosmic wake-up call that is asking us to look at our lives and to begin to make new decisions about our life. When we say, **'YES'** to finding our real meaning and purpose in life, we call forth an inner catalyst that initiates a change in consciousness. When consciousness shifts into a new understanding, a space is created that allows for the birthing of a deeper sense of Self-knowledge. Once consciousness shifts, it is difficult to go back to our former awareness. We either find a greater meaning in whatever it is that we are currently doing or the universe moves us on into something else.

In these cosmic wake-up moments we are moved to edge of mystery. We do not know where we are going or what is going to happen to us, we just know that we cannot stay the same. What we ultimately discover is that the edge of mystery is the place where creativity lives. When we are willing to dance at mysteries edge, we find that this willingness of participation awakens us to a deeper understanding of creativity and co-creation and invites us to enter further into its domain. This domain holds inspired insights, that desire to be aroused, awakened and placed into service in the world and in to a growing our sense of <u>S</u>elf-awareness.

When we choose to apply these inspired insights to the activities of daily living, the effect of this decision ripples out into all areas of our life. As the ripples spread, the circles of our sense of <u>S</u>elf-awareness expands and releases with each new wave, an amplification of the sense of personal responsibility that we carry for our thoughts and actions. With each of these amplifications of thought, the "imprisoned splendor" of the True Self is set free.

"Life is an opportunity to heal, use it well."
— Michael Ryce

Chapter 3
The Circle of 'Transformation': Imagine

"You are the Root <u>Cause</u> of Your Experience"

Stopping Negative Thoughts and Monkey Mind Chatter

As was stated earlier, <u>S</u>elf-discovery is a process of asking the right questions and through this uncovering the deeper truths about who we are and the abilities that we have. When this shift begins to happen we start to realize that we are responsible people who have the power to alter and shape the conditions of our life. We have the power and the right to engage in possibility thinking and begin to imagine something more exciting for our life.

Please note that it is important to remember that when you are in the midst of imagining the possibilities for your future, do not engage in self-blame, self-shame or self-guilt about the past. This is shared, because it is the "nature of the human beast" for these types of thoughts to pop-up. What often occurs when we start to imagine and vision great things for our lives is that negative thoughts begin to arise and try to detract us, or move us away from our heart's desires and goals.

Have you ever heard of monkey-mind chatter (MMC)? MMC is an internal dialogue that announces itself when you about to embark upon something new or take on a new experience. MMC is that voice that says, "There is not any reason to do this. You won't succeed." "You haven't succeeded before, why would you now?" "Remember, they told you wouldn't amount to much, so why try? Prove them right. Don't even put forth the effort."

Are you prone to MMC (monkey-mind chatter)? I know that in my life I have been. In fact, I named my MMC, "Leroy." By doing this I was able to personalize the MMC and talk to it. "OK, Leroy, I heard you, now be quiet! OK, Leroy, I have heard enough about why not to do this."

In order to engage in **S**elf- growth and thus, be able to dream great possibilities into reality, we must learn how to stop this internal mind chatter. MMC is a conversation that says over and over again that you are not enough and/or someone else is to blame for your current predicament.

Blaming others for what "they" have done to you is an escape-route that is commonly used to avoid responsibility for one's own thoughts and actions. Even more, blaming others is a way that you – Give Away Your Power!

Changing the Internal Dialogue

"To change a person must face the dragon
of his appetites..."
—Rumi, translated by Coleman Barks

All of us have an internal dialogue (MMC) going on inside our head. Consciously participating with the **Circle of Transformation** and in **S**elf-discovery process allows us to listen to this inner dialogue (MMC) with "new ears" and then to make changes within our thought-structure or mind-set – by asking new questions. Dreaming about who we can be and what possibilities lie ahead does not include making ourselves guilty for things we have done in the past, but it is about realization. Realizing that we do have the power to do things differently now, if we choose.

Dr. Michael Ryce shares in his book, *Why is this Happening to Me ... Again?* "We are the root-cause of our experiences." The experience is the *effect*, whether we see it or not.

"I am the root cause of my experience."

Realizing the truth of this statement is the first step in finding the source of our empowerment; you are the common denominator *in* and the root cause *of* all of your life experiences. This idea is part of an old axiom which says, "Thoughts held in mind produce after their kind." Or, "What I choose to think about, I become, therefore, if I can change my thoughts I can change my life."

When we begin to practice Self-discovery – truly seeing and realizing what is happening within us and then taking the necessary action in mind to change our thoughts, our lives will begin to shift. When we take charge of what happens inside of our mind, we regain our power. It has been said that we should, "Put away our magnifying glass and get out our mirrors." This means stop magnifying the faults of others. Stop being critical of their behaviors and begin to look in the mirror and focus on ourselves. We can begin by taking an inventory of the major events in our lives that we have perceived as negative and asking ourselves – honestly

– how did we participate in what happened in our life. We cannot say that we are taking responsibility for our life and then continue to blame others for what is happening in our life. It cannot and does not work that way! This may be difficult to understand, but take this in – "You are responsible for your own responses!" "You are response-able."

Thoughts are our vehicle for asking the universe for what we want. However, most of the time, without our conscious awareness, we are asking the universe for what we don't want. So we are creating experiences for our life that we are actually desiring to avoid.

As was stated before, our MMC or inner dialogue is endless. Often we take this chatter and share it with others or we just let it run rampant in our mind, uncontrolled. Either way we are creating destructive mind-energy thought-patterns that will be reflected in our life. For example:

You desire to be prosperous and successful (remember, you always choose what your desire is). Yet when you look at your life, honestly and without blinders, you see that you spend an inordinate amount of time telling your friends, partner and worse yet, yourself, how broke and unsuccessful you really are. What is happening here is that you are focusing the powerful energy you have available to you--your thoughts-- on a negative thought-form instead of a positive, constructive one.

Positive or negative, the universe doesn't care. It will respond to our call. It will attract back to us that which we send forth as a dominant thought or belief. Negative thoughts that we hold about what we don't want are just as powerful as the thoughts we hold about what we do want.

I really believe that there is only a **'YES'** that pulsates throughout the universe. There is not a universal 'NO,' it doesn't exist. What is real, is that whatever we hold as our dominant thought or belief is what we are saying, **'YES'** to as our experience. We can say **'YES'** to our highest good or we can say **'YES'** to anxiety, worry, concern, doubt – and each will attract to us more of the same.

That is why it is so important that we become responsible for our inner-dialogue and our spoken word. This is why great thinkers have always said, "Be careful what you ask for. You might get it!" Impeccable in the type of thoughts, words, and actions we participate in and with. We are responsible for our mind chatter and our thoughts; and we do draw to us the experiences in life that are patterned after those thoughts and beliefs that we hold. And those experiences will continue to repeat themselves until we choose to change the underlying causal thought.

Imagine This – Conscious Choice Creates Conscious Transformation

It has been said that choice is at the center of the evolutionary process and the engine of our evolution. Over the centuries people have made conscious, responsible choices. Choices that invited them to continue with and follow through on their theories, discoveries, models, concepts, ideas, notions, hunches, inventions, schemes, assumptions, etc., and through these choices they have catapulted humankind from the Dark Ages to an age of advanced scientific and spiritual development not even considered 150 years ago.

What is a conscious, responsible choice and how do we know when we are making one? A responsible choice occurs when we take into account the consequences that our choices will have, not just on us, but on others also. Inherent in conscious, responsible choices are the following questions:

"What will be the consequences of this choice?"

"Am I willing to live with the consequences?"

"Is this outcome what I ultimately want to create in my life?"

"Am I willing to accept the outcome of my choice?"

"Will any one be hurt, angered, feel cheated, etc., by my choice of response in this moment?"

"If yes, am I willing to consciously hurt, anger, cheat, etc., someone?"

"After all is taken into consideration, is this what I really want?"

At this point we are only asking the question to see what we think and how we feel, looking to see what might happen as a result of our actions; we are not holding any intentions.

If it is what you really want, then go for it! Say, '**YES**'! If it isn't, then wait until the timing is right. In this way we are staying conscious and making responsible choices. These actions feed the heart and soul and our feelings of self-esteem. When we feel good about ourselves it easier the next time to make the next conscious, responsible choice and then each choice begins to lead us onto the path of conscious transformation and authentic power.

The choices we make in any given situation depend upon how well we know ourselves. We may desperately want to be kind, but our vicious nature may be stronger. If we are not conscious of all of the different aspects of ourselves, the part of our self that is the strongest will prevail. Thus, the intention of our vicious nature, to control and manipulate people, will be the one that the personality uses to create its reality.

Whether we realize it or not, our choices have at their foundation intention. For instance, choosing to speak up or not has the possibility of making a decision based on several different intentions. We may choose to remain silent because our intention is punishment. Or, our intention may be to choose to speak with authority tempered by anger in order to scare someone. We may choose to speak softly and sweetly because we intend to show compassion, or how much we love someone. Each thought and action holds the intention of the quality of consciousness that is brought to the thought or action.

This is why conscious choice, made in conjunction with conscious intentions is so important. We cannot choose our intentions consciously until we become aware of the different aspects of ourselves. When we are not conscious of these aspects or natures we find ourselves in the situation where we end up lamenting the outcomes of conditions and situations, because what we experienced was not what we intended to have happen. We thought that things would go in one direction and they went in another.

You may be aware that deception is not in integrity with how you want to live, but you make the decision that in order to be sales person of the month you will commit an act of deception – such as over-selling a customer a product that will become obsolete before they could use all of it up.

How do you know when your choices and intentions are in alignment? Choices made in conjunction with positive intentions are in alignment with the heart and they result in leaving you with a sense of "ahhh," or a feeling or thought of '**YES**', we all win, I feel good, this was right; and the outcome yielded love, forgiveness, compassion, clarity, grace, ease and more.

Choices made through I win, you lose or through a sense of anger, fear, jealousy, deception, and so forth, leave us feeling temporarily high and then deflated, wondering, feeling guilt or shame, and ultimately powerless. We gain or lose a sense of internal power-filledness according to the choices we make.

When we consciously make the decision to invoke growth, to know more of who we really are, we are consciously saying '**YES**' to opening the doors of the mind and heart to internal revelation. We are asking that those aspects of ourselves, which are ready to be whole and healed, come forth for inspection and healing. What happens next is that with each incidence of fear, deception, anger, fitfulness, jealousy, greed, lust, etc., that comes into our awareness or experience, we are given the choice as to if we will respond or react to it. If we take a moment to consider the consequences of our actions or take a deep breath, we can respond consciously. If we tear right in, we are probably going to react, and go unconscious blaming others for our need to react.

A YES Experience: Imagine Responding in New Ways

Reinforcement through Repetition:

The choices we make in any given situation depend upon how well we know ourselves. We may desperately want to be kind, but our vicious nature may be stronger. If we are not conscious of all of the different aspects of ourselves, the part of our self that is the strongest will prevail. Thus, the intention of our vicious nature, to control and manipulate people, will be the one that the personality uses to create its reality.

Have you ever had to go into a meeting with someone you did not trust or like? You gave yourself a pep talk, told yourself things would be different this time, you would behave differently, you definitely would stay calm, etc. The meeting begins and "the other one" starts with their whining, complaining, and self-absorbed behavior. You see yourself starting to get agitated and you tell yourself, "I am calm. I release and let this go." Suddenly you find that you are "hooked" and you begin to react to this other person's behavior. You walk out of the meeting wondering what just happened.

Please think of a similar situation, as to the one stated above and then answer the following question.

My need to be _____ became stronger than my need to be _____.

Example:

My need to be (seen as his/her equal) / (in control) became stronger than my need to be (generous of spirit) / (forgiving).

A 'YES' Experience: Imagine Slaying the Green-Eyed Monster

You are with your partner and a good-looking "ex" that your partner used to date comes up and starts to flirt with him/her. You have a moment of choice! You can get mad and stomp off, start a fight, or, you can stop, take a breath and silently respond to yourself with; "I know who you are Mr. Green Eyed Monster (jealousy), I have danced with you many times before. But now I choose not to engage. I choose to take another deep breath and own my power."

Now think of a situation that you are currently involved in and consider how you might start responding rather than reacting when you are in the midst of it.

(Caution – this experience could change your life!)

WOW! You are learning to make choices based upon the intention to grow. This can only reap feelings of personal strength and power, instead of feeling like a victim and powerless in situations. If your actions, based on your choices, did not require responsibility of choice through self-discipline and positive intention, of what consequence would they be? How would you grow?

Any one can make irresponsible, unconscious choices. Only true winners (in the greater cosmic sense) have the fortitude to make responsible, conscious choices – that ultimately lead to soul growth and healing.

Remember, <u>not to choose</u> is a choice. It can work for us or against us based on why we are making the choice and what the intention is behind the choice. Often we choose not to make a choice because we want to remain unconscious and in an avoidance pattern. Once you start on the path of '**YES**', of awakening to who you are, each decision you make will require that you consciously choose which aspects of your personality you want to integrate today, and in this moment. This is not easy and yet once the journey is embarked upon it is difficult to turn back. For once you start to change, through making conscious choices, you will not want to live in any other way.

Regardless of our negative behaviors and /or addictions – and they come with many faces – we have the power within us to overcome them. We have the ability to say, '**YES**', to something greater for our lives:

Conscious Transformation through Authentic Actions .

Imagine Poss – I – bility

Here is a question to ponder. What is at the center of possibility? Stop and think about this before you read on.

I, the letter I, is at the center of poss-I-bility. Think about this. What could this mean to you and for you? Could it mean that anything is possible when I am willing to put myself into it and be responsible for my thoughts and actions? In addition, if I add intention and creative passion to poss-I-bility, would I have the potential formula for success?

When we live from an attitude that says everything has poss-I-bility; then we can work towards making that which was seemingly impossible – possible. For when our attitudes shift from being negative – not going to happen –to being open to poss-I-bility, we begin to have hope for the future and can see how I am able to make this impossibility happen. Remember, nothing is impossible to those who believe.

Holding the space for possibility, we can move from – impossible, can't be done – to if I place some of my energy into this, then the im-possible moves to I can do this!

Impossibility thinking comes from our 'adverse' ego and it companion, monkey mind chatter. The adverse ego is that part of our personality that holds the idea that "I am not enough," "I am not worthy", etc. I'm possibility in action; comes from having quieted the monkey mind chatter and is a fruit of Self-awareness. Knowing I am possibility in action - comes from be aware of who we are and trusting in our capabilities.

Below are words that connote, not able or not enough, in some manner. Let us take them and shift them into a positive direction.

Example:

Impossibility --> I'm possibility --> I am possiblity

*NOTE: Watch your body responses as you work with these words.

Imbalance	I'm-	I am
Immature	I'm-	I am
Immovable	I'm-	I am
Impolite	I'm-	I am
Impotent	I'm-	I am
Improper	I'm-	I am
Impure	I'm-	I am
Impatient	I'm-	I am

Once you have completed the above, select the word that created the greatest body response and ask yourself: "What desires to be more fully uncovered or discovered about this word/statement that is for my personal growth?"

Write your responses here or in your journal.

_____

_____

_____

_____

A 'YES' Experience: Imagine Liberation from Limitation

Purpose: To engender a sense of personal empowerment, which liberates one to do their highest and best work.

Setting: This can be done alone, as individual work or in pairs. Have gentle music playing in the background.

Materials: Large pieces of paper, personal journals, burning bowl materials, masking tape, crayons or colored pencils.

Life demands a constant flow of creativity. Some aspect of creativity is used when you are figuring out your grocery list, deciding what you are going to buy for your best friend's birthday, choosing how are you going to make a living, reviewing what stocks you should invest in, or asking the question, "Who am I?".

When we feel on top of our game, that's no problem. But if we are unsure of ourselves we make mistakes – everybody does. Or, if we are under stress, doubt begins to erode our confidence. Our creative juices can be slowed to a trickle or even turned off by a little voice inside that whispers, "You're not enough" or "You just don't have it any more." We begin to wonder if we've lost our creative edge.

Negative experiences and events that pile up over time create self-doubt as a basic core – belief that unconsciously colors our creativity and decisions. These limiting negative core beliefs kick in when we are trying to prove ourselves. When we fall short of the victory or the prize that we have set, it allows that little voice to say, "I told you so. See you're not enough."

"Liberation from Limitation" can help release this old baggage by fostering inner change. It gets the body, mind and spirit involved. The mind accepts the idea of the exercise. The body performs it. The spirit witnesses the process and chooses to change.

You will need a large piece of paper, like butcher's paper that comes in big rolls. If you do not have a large roll of butcher paper, you can use an 8½ x 11 piece of paper and draw a large empty heart that fills the paper.

If you are using the butcher block paper cut the paper into strips that are long enough to match your height. **Place the paper** on the wall with masking tape. Draw your silhouette, as best you can, on the paper or, if this is done in a group, a partner can draw the silhouette.

Select your favorite colors of crayons or pencils and draw a large heart in the region of your heart on your silhouette. Spend a short time in quiet reflection just looking at the "empty" heart. If something comes forth draw or write it on the heart. Questions you might ask yourself are:

1. How does creative potential express itself through me?

2. I remember a time when I felt alive and joyful – what was I doing?

3. What does my heart want to reveal or share with me?

4. How do I use my power for good?

5. What would fill my heart and make me happy?

6. Other: _____

Do not try to foresee the answer, do not try to concentrate. Surrender and allow the answers to bubble up from the subconscious. After contemplating these questions for awhile, request that your Higher Self reveal a symbol to you that represents wholeness for your being. Write or draw the word or symbol in the heart and color it.

Allow yourself to be guided from that quiet place within you; after you have completed this experieince, record in your journal the feelings or thoughts that arose during the experience. After you have completed writing your reflections, review everything that has been revealed to you and contemplate the significance of your answers.

"Reality is not as reality is, reality is as we perceive it."
— Thoreau

Chapter 4
The Circle of 'Transformation': Innovate

"Reality is <u>Not</u> as Reality is..."

Shifting Perceptions Creates New Realities

In order to innovate and plan a positive, creative, energy-filled future we need to learn how to shift our perception of reality, so that we are not continuing to create more of the same old, same old. Perception is defined as *"an internal, made-up story which is externalized or overlaid on the actual world."* Every thought we hold in mind or, it might be better said that every perception of reality that we hold, sets up an energy wave to attract people (and conditions) who are in tune with that perception of reality.

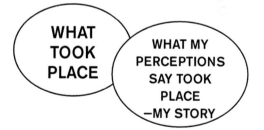

The people or situations we attract help us to fulfill our future according to our dominant thoughts. The outer experience does not cause our feelings or beliefs; that person or situation only resonates with that which is already present within us. What does this mean?

Two examples:

1. No one can make us angry. We perceive the situation as heated and then allow our feelings to flow in the direction of anger.

2. I may perceive an incident as something that is not worthy of fighting over, yet someone else may perceive the same type of incident as something they are willing to die for. The difference between the two is our perception of reality and the choices we make around that perception.

Whenever we put thought-energy – energy that has been held over a period of time with an intensity – such as hate, distrust, low self-esteem thoughts – into our cellular structure or physiology, we create a corresponding feeling for that thought-energy. Feelings are the body's feedback mechanism that lets us know whether we are engaging in constructive or destructive mind-energy.

When we participate long enough in destructive mind-energy (such as being angry all the time or feeling sorry for ourselves) the body will eventually create some form of somatic dis-ease (burning sensation in the stomach, lower back pain, etc.), to let us know that enough is enough. It is time to look at new ways of being, it is time to consciously design a new future.

The heart is always talking to the intellect or conscious mind via the feeling experience. However, most of us just ignore the signals and go on our merry way continuing in the same destructive thought energy patterns until our body or the world gives us the cosmic 2 x 4 wake-up call that we cannot ignore.

Energy doesn't lie and neither will it be ignored, forever! It will and does make itself known. When we begin to take charge of what is happening inside of us – "*Cause*"— we reap a sense of empowerment in the world – "*Effect*." Thoughts held in mind (Cause) do produce in the outer after their kind (Effect). The information that is available to our mind is limited by our mind-set. For example:

When you are in an argument with someone you care deeply about and you are very angry at them; do you, in that moment, remember all the things that you admire, enjoy or love about them? The answer is, "No." For in that moment of anger or anxiety you are disconnected from feeling your admirable or loving thoughts about them. You are in that moment choosing to engage with them on another level, but do not be deluded that they are the cause, for you are choosing how you will respond to the moment. Thus, you are respon-able.

The intellectual mind limits the information we can receive based on our foundational thought structure. If our foundational thought structure contains the reality perception of, "I must have my way." "They always leave." "Anger is the way to get what I want." Then that is where we will go in our mind, to that belief structure we hold and we will experience the feelings associated with that belief. Feelings are known to be our primary feedback mechanism for the body.

Through **S**elf-discovery we can create a new reality for our life. We can condition the mind with a new set of truths; principles that are steeped in Love, Peace, Beauty, Joy, Prosperity, knowing "Who I Am," etc. These principles held as thoughts begin to create a new reality. Remember, feelings come from within. No one can make us do anything. They can only trigger the cause of the feelings we hold, let us know if we are connected to our Higher Source and whether that Source is flowing freely through us. If consciousness (our awareness of our perceptions) is causal, then how do we become more aware of consciousness and begin to command cause and effect in our life? In other words, "How can I change my thoughts, in order to change my life experiences?"

A 'YES' Experience: Taking Inventory – What Shaped My Perceptions?

You will need your journal or a sheet of paper for this experience.

1. Create a chronological age list starting with your earliest memory or age 5, then 10, 15, 20, 25, 30, 40, 50 and so on. You may choose to add other significant years. Once you have the chronological outline, ask the following questions:

   What were the positive major events of my life at that age?

   If any, write the event or issue next to the corresponding age bracket.

   What were the negative major events of my life at that age?

   If any, write the event or issue next to the corresponding age bracket.

2. After you have this completed the exercise, review the list.

   Do you see any repeating patterns?

   If so, how have they effected your perception of life and how you show up in life?

Example:

1.Ages

    5   Mom and dad divorced, mom left

  10 My best friend moved away

  20 My dog died

  30 Dad remarried and I left home

  40 I was divorced

2. Repeating Pattern/s:

    Pattern:

        People leave me or I leave them.

    How did this affect me?

        I do not let people get close to me. I always hold something back. I don't trust easily.

3. Now that you see these patterns (both positive and negative) and the impact each has had on your life, you can begin to make new choices as to how you view life and how you want to show up.

Create one new goal to begin to shift an old worn-out attitude.

I will _____.

e.g., I will look at my reactions when I start to feel the need to withdraw and begin to ask myself healthy questions about my behavior, such as:

"What purpose is this reaction serving?"

"How can I make this a win/win/win situation?"

"What do I really want in my life?"

"What do I want to design as my future outcomes?"

A 'YES' Experience: Innovate – How Big Do You Dare to Dream?

This next experience advances us towards our goal. It is about innovating, initiating, and implementing your desires. As you participate in this experience, stay open to possibility. Answer the questions without any concern about not being seen as humble, for this moment you are playing really 'big.'

Imagine it is five years from now and your possibilities have unfolded. You are to giving thanks for everything that has been implemented in your life; everything that has come to pass; and everyone who has assisted. List everything (so dare to imagine big) that has happened to you in the past five years to create this miracle life. Now, speak it out loud!

"Passion is your verve for life. Pass it on."
— TGB

Chapter 5
The Circle of 'Transformation': Implement

Intention, Direction, & Attention Aligned With Focus, Clarity, & Purpose Create Authentic Actions

What Am I Implementing?

What do I need to implement in my life that will shift the outcomes of my experiences? This is a 'right' question and in order to answer it let us look at – what implement means?

To Implement:

> **Noun** 1. **Tool:** *useful article of equipment, usually a specially shaped object to do a particular task* 2. **Requirement:** *something needed in order to achieve something*

> **Verb** 1. **Carry out or fulfill:** *to put something into effect or action give tools* 2. **Give tools to:** *to provide or equip somebody with the tools or other means to do something* [160]

Who am I? What is my potential? What capabilities do I have that I am not using, maximizing, or exercising?

Did you know that successful people are risk-takers? What are you willing to risk in order to move to the next level, to reach the next goal? Do you have what it takes to risk letting go of co-dependency, fear, limited thinking, status quo, and others conditioned thoughts about who you are? Are you ready to implement the changes needed in your life? Are you ready to say '**YES**' to that which has the potential to shift the outcomes of your future experiences?

Throughout this book ideas and practical tools have been given that can provide and equip you with the means to create and implement something different for your life – if you choose. We have learned about listening to our intuition, to watch for what it is that is nudging us and desiring to take us in new directions. When we say, '**YES**' to the nudge we are taking our first step on the journey through the *Circle of Transformation.*

Where the *Circle of Transformation* ultimately moves us is to the place of choice and decision making – do we dare implement, through taking authentic actions – what we have imagined and innovated as goals, dreams, desires, and as our future? Are we ready to say, '**YES**' and to move forward in implementing our ideas? Remember, we can have anything we choose

A 'YES' Experience: Shifting Behavior Patterns

This experience is a question that you are to reflect upon. Not just for a minute and then moving on, but take some time for deep reflection – it could shift your behavior patterns. You say you are ready to change, yet when you are given specific tools to work with, you choose to ignore them, or use them for a day and then say, "Oh well, that didn't work."

Is this type behavior, trying a tool for one day or one time, truly about saying '**YES**' to something greater happening in your life? Does it leave room for the possibility of possibility to unfold itself? What can you do to keep yourself on track? What would it take for you to remain consciously engaged? What is really holding you back from experiencing your highest good?

(Be honest with your answers! The only one you will or can fool, is yourself. Honesty is the prelude to experiencing true _S_elf-observation and _S_elf-awareness.)

Intention – What Did I Really Intend to Do?

"As a man thinks in his heart, so is he."
— Proverbs 23:7

There was a question posed in one of the earlier chapters, it was, "How can I change my thoughts, in order to change my life experiences?" Although we have shared many ideas on this subject throughout the book, there is one more that needs to be discussed. It is the concept of change as revealed through intention, attention, and the direction of the mind. Through understanding the basics of these three concepts and implementing them as practical activities of everyday life, we can begin to bring conscious change into our environment.

Intention: What is my true intention, in every situation in which I participate?

Attention: Where am I keeping the focus of my attention? Are my thoughts clear and focused?

Direction: Upon what am I directing the direction of my mind?

These ideas require us to look closely and honestly at the intent of our intentions, the focus of our attention including the clarity of our thoughts, and the compatibility of our actions and thoughts in accordance with the direction in which we say we are heading.

Let us begin by exploring intention. Intention is defined as, *that which we plan to do or that which we plan as an outcome to a situation.* Intention sets the tone for what we do and gives us a direction for outcome. "I intend to ...." Awareness (or conscious mind) is conditioned by intention. In any given situation that we are involved in, what are we really and truly intending to do? The answer to this question requires that we be extremely honest with ourselves.

Think of a problem situation that you are in the midst of resolving. Ask yourself, "Am I intending to be open and honest in this situation, letting everyone have their say?" Or, "Am I intending to control and manipulate the situation while looking like I am being benevolent and kind?" This is **S**elf-honesty at its most impeccable nature.

The energy of the true intention that we hold goes forth to attract back to us "in kind." It will return to us as we have given it out. We may be gleeful that we have just out-maneuvered someone, it may seem in the moment that we have over-powered someone, out witted someone, or gotten our way through the power of our intellect – but as "they" say – Captain Karma always win!

e.g., You decide to give your son $500. But behind

this outer act of giving is the inner thought; "Now he will be indebted to me and will do what I want him to do." This act was not done with a spirit of pure intention. It had strings attached.

Intention aligned with purity, love and harmlessness draws to us love, joy, peace, health and understanding. Mis-aligned intention draws to us pain, confusion, hurt, misunderstanding, and frustration. If these latter conditions are revealing themselves in our life, they are signals from the universe that something in our thinking needs to shift, change or be re-aligned.

A 'YES' Experience: My Intention Was To ...

Ask your self, with a sense of total honesty, to think about a situation that created havoc for you – in other words the outcome did not match your expectations.

The situation was:

_____

"My intention, in this situation, was to ...

_____

The results were:

_____

Could it be that your intentions were not actually in alignment with the highest and best for all, but, were skewed towards getting things done my way or having the outcome I wanted?

BE HONEST! _S_elf-honesty is a prelude to awakening to _S_elf-awareness and to awakening to deeper understandings.

Write the answer to the question on this page or in your journal, then reflect on it again, until you feel clear that all your intentions (positive and negative) have been expressed. Intend to know your true thoughts and feelings. Intend to change. Only you can change you. Intend to do so.

Before I start any project, class, book, counseling or spiritual coaching session I set an intention for that experience. I consciously surrender my way or my will to whatever is the Greater Good of the Universe. I am very clear that I may not know what the ultimate Good or outcome may be for me or anyone else.

I believe that surrender is the act of making one's self available to be in and of the flow of the Universal Energy. I also know that this Energy is desiring in every moment to move through me individually and each of us, collectively. When we surrender and hold the Greater Good of a situation as our intention and we are moving our personal little ego aside, we open the way for wonderful things to happen. For what we have created in this act of surrender is a conscious conduit for Good.

It has also been said that holding intention is akin to being in-tension, like a string on a guitar. When a guitar string is in-tension it can be played. When it is not, nothing can be played. Intention, helps make us instruments of the Universal Energy, waiting to be played.

Attention – On What Am I Focusing?

"Though we seem to be sleeping there is an inner wakeful-
ness that directs the dream, and that will eventually startle
us back to the truth of who we are."
—Rumi, translated by Coleman Barks

Where attention goes energy flows. Wherever we allow our mind to roam our energy will follow. The problem is that we may be expending a lot of energy in the 'wrong' direction. An example of this is when we allow our mind to follow anxiety, worry, concern, doubt, or fear. It costs a lot to keep these hooligans as traveling companions. It costs us peace of mind, joy, a sense of calm, and so much more. It isn't worth it. Use affirmations; keep bringing your attention back on what you want, and not on what you don't want. The Law says, where we keep thoughts will determine what reveals itself in our life. This is the power of Attention.

Attention is the art of being aware of what is showing up in our life and recognizing how we respond to it. It is also, about being aware of where we are focusing our thoughts. This is not about blame, shame or guilt, this is about what is and what is – is that we have the power to keep our mind focused on that which is most important to us. It just takes training and discipline – practical application.

Most of us have spent time investing our energy in the belief that someone or something out there has power over us. After all, they are – more successful than us, or, they are the boss, our partner, the rich and famous, or just some one we perceive as being greater than we are. But, in actuality, no one has power over us that we don't give them. We are responsible for our lives. Believe it!

85

A 'YES' Experience: A Stretch!

Now that you have learned how to involve yourself with the Power of '**YES**' you are invited to participate in an experience that involves saying '**YES**' and meaning it; you are being asked to stretch.

If you would, and if you physically are able, please raise your right arm and hold it way up in the air. Now, raise your left arm and hold it way up in the air. Now reach higher.

What are you doing? You are stretching and in the course of stretching, you are physically creating the **Y** in '**YES**.' As you stretch and create the physical **Y**, you are also participating in the spiritual act of opening yourself to be a container or chalice for the Universal Energy to move through.

There are no blocks over you heart space, or any where else, you are wide open. Open, receptive, and ready to receive; remember this if you come to a rough spot and do not know where to turn. Just stop, breath, and raise you arms into the Universal symbol of '**YES**.'

It appears that on the physical level you are stretching however, on the spiritual level this will trigger an invitation for new energy to move through you. Be observant; stay alert, for you will receive a nudge, push, or intuitive hit. Be ready to move and to take authentic action.

Are you ready to participate in this next experience? The Power of '**YES**' invites you to stretch, to reach a little higher, to enlarge and broaden your realms of possibilities. With this thought in mind you are invited to create a stretch. What are you willing to say, '**YES**' to this week, that will encourage you to stretch into new arenas and/or awareness' about your self or others? What do you want to do, but have been to busy (procrastinating) to do? It doesn't have to be difficult or complex, it just has to be a stretch. Write your stretch here – don't forget to make it S.M.A.R.T.

_____

_____

When you have completed your stretch exercise find someone to share your accomplishments with; a partner in growth that will support you in your joy and in your journey to wholeness.

Direct Your Mind and You Direct Your Life

*"Observe the wonders as they occur around you.
Don't claim them. Feel the artistry
moving through, and be silent"*
—Rumi, translated by Coleman Barks

Learning to take charge of our thoughts is not an easy task, for we are conditioned to allow the mind to wander where it will. The mind is actually like an undisciplined child. However, there is good news. With a little discipline, we can shift the mind into assuming the role it was intended to have – that of an instrument that can be used to positively co-create our lives rather than creating upset and anxiety.

The word direction refers to the direction of our mind and where we let our thoughts take us. What fields do we let our mind wander in? Do we let our mind run rampant with all kinds of made-up negative scenarios? Do we allow negative monkey-mind chatter to work us into a frenzy? Do we continually worry about things that never happen? Reflecting honestly, through-out the day, are these the thought patterns that consume and run our mind? If they are, how can we learn to focus our mind in a direction that is positive, uplifting, and heading us towards a greater good?

For instance:

Have you ever had something happen to you that you wanted to forget it, but your mind would not let it go? In fact, your mind kept running the scenario until you found yourself in a state of turmoil and anxiety?

We can learn to take command of our thoughts, moving them into directions that we want to stay focused on. As was stated earlier, in the beginning this not an easy task, but it can be accomplished in a relatively short amount of time – as long as we hold an intention, along with a commitment, to do so. Through the following venues we can begin focusing the mind, quieting the MMC (monkey-mind chatter), and learn how to hold the trickery of the mind at bay. We accomplish this through:

Daily prayer and contemplation

Daily meditation

Taking personal contemplation and silence retreats

Right use of affirmations

Being clear of our intentions

Practicing Self-observation and Self-discovery

Making conscious choices

Spiritual counseling and/or coaching

Reading self-help and spiritual books, and listening to motivational CD's.

Attending classes, work-shops, lectures, and self-help seminars.

Forming or finding groups of like-minded people

Prayer, along with contemplation, initiates the act of stilling of the mind, as it focuses the mind on a single thought or scripture (See Presence Pause.). Meditation completes the act of stilling the mind as it opens the way, through Silence and Receptivity, for a greater amount of Universal Energy to move through you. Along with this, the act of taking time apart, such a personal silent retreat is very good for inner discovery.

Affirmations are positive statements that we repeat over and over until we start to recognize their wisdom. "I am open and receptive to Higher Wisdom." "I am beautiful, inside and out." "I am the master of my ship, responsible for my direction." "Life is good, I am good, and all is good."

Intention, Self-observation and conscious choice (the act of making choices responsibly and with full awareness of ones actions and possible consequences) are described in other chapters.

A coach, be it a mentoring type for a specific area of work or a spiritual coach, can help one move along the path of <u>Self-discovery</u> more quickly and with less drama. As a spiritual coach, I have found that people are less likely to participate in negative behaviors when they have made a commitment to showing up in integrity. Coaching alters the behaviors and opens the client to new avenues of awareness. For coaching to work, the client must be ready to initiate change in their life, even if it is only a baby-step.

<u>Classes, workshops and joining small groups</u> are always a good idea when one is initiating a new adventure on the spiritual path. Groups and classes, etc., hold an inherent power of helping one to attain a higher perspective. This perspective can come from what is taught and learned from the facilitator, the other members, and of course, from the willingness to share one's own story and experiences. As Rev. Johnny Coleman says, *"It works if you work it."*

A 'YES' Experience: Seven Authentic Actions:
A 30 Day Plan

For the next thirty days, I commit to using at least two of these authentic actions per week.

1. I will, on a daily basis, create and ask at least three 'right' questions. Questions that are designed to lead me to a greater sense of who I am.

2. I will, on a daily basis, work with at least two of the tools and techniques; and honestly observe what difference they make in my life.

3. I will, on a daily basis, refer to the Laws/Principles and consciously apply at least one of them to the situations occurring in my life.

4. I will, on a daily basis, watch my words and tell my monkey mind chatter to hush up and move on.

5. I will, on a daily basis, create affirmations that affirm my self-worth.

6. I will, on a daily basis, assess my thoughts, words, and actions and be clear that they reflect what I want to produce in my life. If they do not, I will do an exercise to shift them.

7. I will, on a daily basis, journal my thoughts, reactions, responses, etc. in order to discover more about my self. I will make one new discovery about myself a day.

*Authentic Actions are always S.M.A.R.T.

(Specific, Measurable, Attainable, Relative & Time-specific)

A 'YES' Experience: A Presence Pause

*Take time to be present with the Inner-Presence
and the world around you will reflect that honoring.*

—TGB

Is there something currently bothering you, that perhaps your mind has run away with – a thought that is creating anxiety and upset for you? I would invite you to participate in this experience entitled, A Presence Pause. Start to engage this practice as a part of your journey to finding inner peace and tranquility.

Purpose: To center oneself in the midst of a chaotic day, or for inspiration, empowerment or clearing.

Setting: Individual inner-work that can be done at home, in an office or in a group with a facilitator.

Materials: Chairs, soft background music, candles and journals (optional).

The stresses of life, piled day upon day, can take a toll on our mental clarity and the energy we have for creativity. We tend to focus on the past and on the future, and let the present slide away from us. The "Presence Pause" will help you to stay emotionally centered and mentally sharp by stilling the mind and body and turning attention to the moment. The only change we can make is in the present.

The "Presence Pause" has four easy steps:

1. Stop.

Take a time out. Put your work aside. Just stop what you are doing and get comfortable in a chair with your feet flat on the floor and your arms at rest. (This doesn't have to be an ordeal, make it as simple as possible – you could do this on an elevator.)

2. Breathe.

Close your eyes and breathe in through the nostrils slowly and deeply to the count of four. Feel the belly contract and then expand along with the breath. Hold the breath for a moment and then release it slowly to the count of four. Be mindful of the breath and how it moves through the body.

3. Focus.

As you continue to breathe slowly and evenly, imagine a gentle stream that is flowing effortlessly. Occasionally a leaf floats by, gently and easily carried by the flow of the water. The leaves represent any thoughts that may come forth seeking your attention. Let the thoughts, no matter how important, be carried down the stream by the gentle flow of the water. Focus on the word "Peace." Think it silently and gently over and over: "Peace, Peace, Peace..."

4. Release.

If any other thought comes forth, imagine it is a leaf on the stream, floating away. See the word

"Peace" written on the leaf as it flows away. With each breath, feel your self letting go of all concerns, outside influences and thoughts. Release the thoughts and let them drift away, replaced by the essence of Peace.

Consciously focus on the breath and continue to breathe easily and rhythmically. Life began with breath, and we can return to a state of inner-quiet by focusing on the rhythmic movement of our own breathing. With the mind focused inward, continue to relax through the activity of breathing.

As you become quieter and quieter you will now notice that you are able to hear your own inner voice speaking to you. In this state of quiet contemplation, you will be guided and directed as to what you are to do now or what you are to do next. When you are ready, gently, and easily return your thoughts to the present moment.

Other words can be used in place of Peace: Love, Joy, Happiness, Harmony, and so on. If you do this exercise periodically, you will find yourself choosing different words that match your needs. When this exercise is complete, please take time to journal any thoughts that may have come to you.

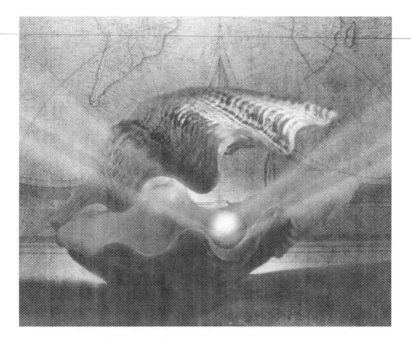

Epilogue: Soul- Searching's

M
ay these writings, in the form of odes and poems, which brought a healing balm to my soul and ultimately to my life, bring the same energy to you; as you engage with their deeper essence. Each ode or poem is set-up under a heading of the topic they relate to; e.g., writings on change and the fear that envelops us while we are in the midst of that change, are listed under the heading Change and Fear.

Please read these odes with an open heart and mind; being willing to dance at the edge of mystery with them as they move you towards new depths of awareness.

A 'YES' Experience: Healing Waters

On Change and Fear:

*To dance with life, means
that I must be willing to
move my feet.*
*To move my feet means that
I must be willing to shift
positions.*
*To shift positions means
that I must be willing to
change.*

*Why would I retreat into the
familiar when
I know possibility awaits me
in moving forward?*

*Why am I so comfortable
In that which causes me so
much pain?*

*Why would I allow fear
To be the ruler of my
household,
When I know it is such
a liar?*

*Rumi says,
"...The thief came in and
took all but the moonlight
in the window."*
*I realize now that things
come and go,*
*People come and go, jobs
come and go,*
*But can the Real ever be
taken from me?*

*Fear has taught me many
things,*
*One of which is that I do not
want to be associated
with it any longer.*

What am I afraid of?
Why would I believe "fear"
*When I know it has not told
me the truth*
*Or, served me well in the
past?*

Does my destiny lie in
forging ahead
Or, in going back?

He told me that I did not
have what it takes to ...
The thief tried to steal my
self-esteem
And through the appearance
of violation
I found Grace and Glory.

Worry is a thief
Who steals your peace
And leaves anxiety
As its calling card.

Riptides, they look like
innocent streaks upon the
water;
Get caught in one and fight
its hidden current
And you will go under.
Relax, swim with it,
And you will survive;
For it will carry you safely out
of its fury.
Isn't this a lesson for me on
how to respond
When fear overwhelms me?

I die to one aspect of life
In order that I might live more
fully in another.

The old and new collide and
I am caught in the center of
the two.
It feels like I am breaking
down but
Am I really being born anew?

If you want to travel far,
quickly,
Then don't take much
baggage.
Worry, anxiety, fear, concern,
jealousy, greed, and envy
Tend to weigh you down and
Thus, do not make great
traveling companions.

Miscellaneous Musings:

Do you know who I am?
Neither do I.
That is why I am here.

Who says you can't dance?
The real question is –
Can they hear the rhythm
To which you are dancing?

To die is to live.
To die a thousand deaths has
*   the inherent gift*
Of the ability to live a
*   thousand new lives.*
Ah, then each negative
*   thought, belief, and/or*
*   experience I choose to*
*   release*
Has the ability to teach me a
*   new lesson and*
Take me in a new direction.
What am I waiting for?

The Teacher had just
*   completed a discourse*
On Wisdom's Feast and the
*   student queried,*
"How shall I live when the
*   time comes*
When nothing brings me
*   pleasure anymore?"*
The Wise One responded,
"Live in excited anticipation,
For when that time comes
You are ripe for Life to live
*   you."*

Regardless of what the
*   experiences of life*
*   bring on,*
The Real never leaves us, nor
*   is lost.*

Who am I, if I am not
(Lover, teacher, mother, sister,
business entrepreneur, ...)
For I am nothing without my
*   labels,*
Or, at least that is what I
*   have been taught.*
Work, strive, attain!
... What if it has all been a
*   lie?*

Hu, Hu, Allah!
Hu means life.
Allah means God, the Eternal.
Thus, in the Eternal is true
Life.

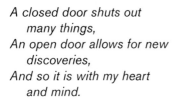

In having nothing to label me
I have no limits to the
    possibility
And potential of who I am.

Leaves blowing in the wind,
Caring not where they fall.
Ah, if I could only trust that
    much.

The day has a thousand
    possibilities,
Choose one!

Let your Higher Spirit guide
    your decisions,
And that same Spirit will go
    forth to prepare the way of
    fulfillment.

A closed door shuts out
    many things,
An open door allows for new
    discoveries,
And so it is with my heart
    and mind.

Crashing waves do not cry,
"Look at me, look at what just
    happened to me."
No, they hit the sand
    – regroup – and
Wait for another opportunity
    to move again.

"Make womb for me, make
    room for me,"
The Divine speaks to my
    heart,
"For you and I are One."

Blue sky meets blue water at
    the edge of the horizon,
Melding, merging, one into
    the other
Until all boundaries are lost
    and they appear as One.
Perhaps this is a sign of what
    can happen to me
When I surrender my
    resistance to that which
    surrounds me.

Birds in flight,
Catching the current
    instinctively and
Flying on it without effort.
If only my instincts
Were that honed.

On Silence:

*For years I have spoken in
order to be heard and
thus feel fulfilled.
In the Silence I have learned
that no words are needed
to Be fully Filled.*

---

*Between the space between
the in-breath and the out-
breath
Lies Eternity and the Eternal
Silence;
Dive in!*

---

*The Great Silence births
us into a world which
teaches us to forget
And once here, through that
same Silence, we again
remember.*

---

*In quietness is your strength
and salvation.
Why then do I run to and fro
trying to find sustenance
and abundance
When through the Silence,
my own will come to me?*

On Emptiness:

*Existence and Emptiness
dance, the longing for one
creates the other.*

---

*Out of Emptiness arises
everything.
Out of Nothingness arises all.*

---

*Safety lies in knowing who
I am.
I am the Eternal Emptiness,
the NO-Thing.
And as NO-Thing,
Nothing can be taken from me.*

*Which has more potential,
The Emptiness of the
Unknown, or,
That which I already know?*

---

*"i" in You (God) and You in
me.
When "i" uncovers You
"i" dissolves into the
Nothingness,
From which it came and
Thus, discovers there was
only You all along.*

Surrendering to the lesson of
sadness,
She is able to hear sadness'
song singing to her.
"Listen to me, listen to me,
I have come to teach you
about yourself."
Surrendering to the lesson of
despair,
She is able to feel despair's
concern for her.
"You have been running to
and fro, going faster and
faster;
Forgetting more and more of
who you really are."
Surrendering to the lesson of
grief,
She is able to touch a place
in her
That childhood experiences
had molded;
Experiences that have been
Chasing her all her life
No matter how fast she ran.
Surrendering to the lessons
of the
(W)holiness inherent in all
that appears –
Sad/Happy, Joy/Despair,
Grief/Gratefulness –
She emerges from the
darkness, In-lightened.

In silent contemplation she
sits,
And as Sacred Emptiness
fills her,
Love flows from her heart
into every cell of her
being.
This Love is a healing balm
that she drinks in,
For it feels like droplets of
rain that have found
Their way to parched and
thirsty ground.
With them come a new hope
For a vibrant and fertile
Spring.
Yes, Love is doing a mighty
work in her,
For It is creating a moist and
verdant place
Where thoughts of Truth can
grow and ripen
Into maturity and then into
manifestation.

If I and God are One,
and because of this you and
I are One,
then I ask you –
is the One doing the writing
and the One doing the
reading, the same One?
"Yes?" Ah, then that is why is
feels like this was written
for me.

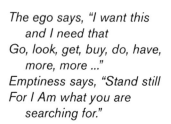

The ego says, "I want this
    and I need that
Go, look, get, buy, do, have,
    more, more ..."
Emptiness says, "Stand still
For I Am what you are
    searching for."

Cast your net into the
    Emptiness and
See what lies within to be
    brought forth.

**On Passion, Love, and the
Beloved:**

Passion,
Pass – I – on
Pass -- the Essence of who
    you are -- on.
Dare to make a difference in
    the world!

It has been said, "Find a void
    and fill it."
The Beloved says,
"Let the **V**oid find you
And you will be filled."

I feel like I am candle flame,
That has been sparked by a
    Sacred Power,
And like a kindling flame
That spreads to share its
    warmth,
My flame spreads to share
    – Love.

Love burns us in Its fire and
Love saves us from the fires.
The results of the two
    experiences are the same,
It is we who differentiate
    between them.

Passion is your verve for life.
It is how you uniquely light
    up the world.
Pass it on.

Who are you to tell me who
    I am?
Are we not both children of
    the Beloved?
If this is so, then this makes
    me your equal –
Regardless, of what you
    think.

Night after night the lover
     waits by the window for
The return of the Beloved.
When at last the Beloved
     appears
They join together in Sacred
     Ecstasy.
And this brief encounter
     gives the lover strength
To return to waiting by the
     window, once more.

❧

As the moonlight does,
I would like to share myself
With you and the world;
Free and unabashed!

❧

Is passion something to be
     hidden?
If yes, what about passion
     needs to hide?
Is passion something to
     revealed?
If yes, who determines how I
     do that?
Why would anyone other
     than my Soul
Be allowed to tell me
What to do with my passion?

In pondering "Union" with the
     Beloved,
I reflect upon mating lizards
     on my back porch,
basking in the sun, frolicking
     to and fro.
She runs and he pursues
     until at last she stops
and they join together in
     union, in oneness.
Bodies entwined, moving to
     the rhythmic flow
Of the eternal dance of the
     universe,
calling forth the essence of
     new life in the process.
How much they remind me of
     myself and my pursuit of
     Oneness with Spirit.
I run to and fro and Spirit
     pursues, ever calling,
"Here I am, let me catch you.
I am what you desire."
Finally I surrender my will
     and stand still,
allowing the sacred Energy
     to penetrate my being,
filling me with the Essence of
     new Life.

*Dance upon my heart, Oh,
    Beloved.
Let the paradoxical rhythm
    of the dance of life con-
    tinually sway me to and
    fro.
A waltz or a jitterbug,
Agony or ecstasy – it
    matters not!
As long as it is Your
    footsteps
That make their Sacred
    Imprint upon my soul.*

*I wait, Oh Beloved,
Desiring that in the
    dance of Life
My dance card be filled
    by You, only.*

On Saying 'YES':

*One morning as I arose
Spirit spoke to me and said,
"You are empowered to do
    great things.
There is a dynamic, creative
    Splendor locked inside
    of you, waiting to be
    unleashed.
The question today is;
Will you say, 'YES'
And allow It to come forth?"*

*A friend once said to me;
"The secret to learning life's
lessons is simple.
Just say, 'yes' and let go."
What she forgot to tell me
    was that "simple" doesn't
    always mean easy.*

*You are destined for success.
The question is not,
What does that success
    look like?
But, will you accept it?*

*How do you live life?
From a state of
"NO, I could never do that."
Or, "I don't deserve that."
Or, do you step up in your
    fullness of glory and say,
"YES, bring it on! Wow,
    I am ready."
When you consciously
    choose to live each day
    from an awareness of
    "YES and WOW," you live
    in awe, wonder and
    joyous expectation and the
    Universe responds
    in kind.*

About the Author

Toni G. Boehm is dynamic, inspirational, motivational speaker and an author, nurse, minister, poet, and teacher of spirituality and mysticism. Throughout her ministerial career, Boehm has held positions as: Dean of Administration, Unity School of Religious Studies; Vice President Education, Unity Institute; Vice President Retreats, Outreach and Special Events, at world headquarters, Unity School of Christianity, Unity Village, MO.

Teaching internationally, she facilitates classes and seminars on personal impowerment, prayer, prosperity, personal growth, awakening the divine feminine in the 21st Century, spiritual transformation and Transformation Coaching©. Boehm introduces students to the spiritual knowledge and skills necessary for living their lives from their highest innate potential. Her life work is devoted to *"being a midwife for the birthing of the soul's remembrance."*

Boehm holds a Bachelor of Arts in Health Care Education, Ottawa University-Kansas, a Masters of Science in Nursing, University of Missouri, and a Ph. D., Religious Studies, American World University, Iowa and Emerson Theological Institute, California. She is a graduate of the University of Kansas Family Nurse Practitioner program and has been certified as an occupational nurse practitioner. Boehm graduated from the Unity School of Christianity School for Religious Studies in 1989 and is an ordained Unity minister.

Boehm lives with her husband, Jay, on a lake in Missouri and enjoys working with paints, crafts, reading, writing, traveling, collecting artifacts and rocks, and being with the grandchildren.

Rev. Boehm is author of numerous articles and the books:

The Spiritual Intrapreneur: Awakening the Power and Potential Within
One Day My Mouth Just Opened: Reverie, Reflections and Rapturous Musings on the Cycles of a Woman's Life
Embracing the Feminine Nature of the Divine: Integrative Spirituality Heralds the Next Phase of Evolution
Luminous Darkness: Recognizing Opposites as Complements

Boehm can be reached at *www.toniboehm.com* or *revtboehm@aol.com* or by contacting the publisher, see copyright page.

The Power of 'YES' Seven Week Study Guide

Basic Format:

Opening prayer or affirmation; ask 'right' questions and allow time for group interaction; perform *A 'YES' Experience/s* (AYE/s).

Week 1: Introduction

What is the Circle of Transformation and how does it work as a transformative tool in your life?

Change begins the moment you dare to ask the 'bigger' questions. What is a 'bigger' question for your life?

AYE/s: An Extraordinary Being; A Stretch

Week 2: Chapter One

How does the historical approach to problem solving differ from the Circle of Transformation's approach?

What does engaging with 'YES' mean for your life?

AYE/s: Dancing at the Edge of Mystery; Igniting the Spark

Week 3: Chapter Two

What are the tools/techniques that resonate with you?

What Laws/Principles do you recognize and use? Are there others?

Define the art of 'right' questioning? Create one.

AYE/s: Self-Awareness -Who am I?; Who Am I - Meditation

Week 4: Chapter Three

What does, 'You are the root cause of your experience' mean?

What is MMC? Do you experience it? How can you change it?

What is a responsible, conscious choice?

AYE/s: Imagine Liberation from Limitation; Learning to Respond in New Ways

Week 5: Chapter Four

Who can make you angry, sad, etc.? Why?

What is perception? How does it relate to what really happened and the story I created?

AYE/s: Taking Inventory; What Shaped My Perceptions; Poss-I-bility

Week 6: Chapter Five

How can you begin to take control of our thoughts?

What is an authentic action? What elements does it contain?

AYE/s: Seven Authentic Actions (discuss each one and how it contributes to transformation and change in a person's life.)

Week 7: Epilogue

Select three Odes or Poems that resonate with you. Share them one at a time and what it is that touched you?

Epilogue: Soul- Searching's

AYE/s: How Big do You Dare to Dream?

ISBN 978-0-9701537-5-3

50000

Printed in the United States
214297BV00001B/8/A